The Black Widow

The Life and Crimes of Griselda Blanco, America's First Billionaire Drug Smuggler

Hugo Clark

© Copyright 2022 - All rights reserved.

The content contained within this book may not be reproduced, duplicated or transmitted without direct written permission from the author or the publisher.

Under no circumstances will any blame or legal responsibility be held against the publisher, or author, for any damages, reparation, or monetary loss due to the information contained within this book, either directly or indirectly.

Legal Notice:

This book is copyright protected. It is only for personal use. You cannot amend, distribute, sell, use, quote or paraphrase any part, or the content within this book, without the consent of the author or publisher.

Disclaimer Notice:

Please note the information contained within this document is for educational and entertainment purposes only. All effort has been executed to present accurate, up to date, reliable, complete information. No warranties of any kind are declared or implied. Readers acknowledge that the author is not engaged in the rendering of legal, financial, medical or professional advice. The content within this book has been derived from various sources. Please consult a licensed professional before attempting any techniques outlined in this book.

By reading this document, the reader agrees that under no circumstances is the author responsible for any losses, direct or indirect, that are incurred as a result of the use of the information contained within this document, including, but not limited to, errors, omissions, or inaccuracies.

Table of Contents

Table of Contents	2
Introduction	5
Chapter 1: A Girl From Cartagena	11
Chapter 2: A Tale of Two Cities	17
Chapter 3: The Myth Begins	26
Chapter 4: Murder and White Powder	34
Chapter 5: Miami's Vice	46
Chapter 6: The Crusade	65
Chapter 7: Legacies	81
Conclusion	89
References	94

This is a True Crime story. It contains descriptions of violence and drug use that some readers may find upsetting.

Introduction

On September 3, 2012, an unassuming elderly woman was shopping at a local butcher in the Belén district of Medellín, Colombia. It had been a relatively quiet day in the city, by this time already a far cry from the tumultuous and violent years of earlier decades. Indeed, the city of Medellín was on the mend. The woman was a frequent patron of this particular butcher shop, at least once a month descending from her luxurious highrise in Medellín's affluent El Poblado district to buy her supply of meat, usually about $150 worth at a time. Standing just barely five feet tall, considerably overweight for her size, and approaching 70 years old, the bulk purchase of assorted meat would have been a heavy load for her. But this was not a weak woman. Nor was this an ordinary woman.

As she was finishing up her shopping and had just paid for her supplies, the roar of a motorcycle engine approached from outside, and stopped dead outside the butcher's shop. As she went to leave, the motorcyclist was entering, still clad in his riding gear and helmet. He looked around the shop until he spotted the habitual, elderly shopper dressed in her white linen and capri pants, with her round, masculine face. He pulled out a handgun he had concealed and shot the woman twice. One bullet hit her in the head, destroying the upper portion of her face. The other went through her upper body near her shoulder. The unknown masked assassin then left, speeding off again on his motorcycle as onlookers panicked and fled. The woman was dead, found laying in her own blood next to her bulk bag of meat and holding a bible to her chest.

This woman was known by many names: The Godmother, The Cocaine Queen, *La Madrina*, Cocaine Cowgirl, Queenpin, The

Black Widow. But her true name, a name known to criminals from Medellín to Miami to California to New York City, was Griselda Blanco Restrepo, one of the most prominent and successful female criminals in history. Like many aspects of Griselda's life, the identity of her killer is uncertain. However, this was a woman who had made countless enemies over the course of her decades-long criminal career, and there is no doubt that her murder was retribution for one of the countless people in both Colombia and the United States that Griselda had left mourning their loved ones. It is unknown exactly how many murders and hits took place under the direct order of Griselda Blanco, but best estimates suggest upwards of 250.

Griselda Blanco was not an average drug smuggler, and the death toll she exacted was not surprising, given what we know of her character. She was ruthless, ambitious, and cold. She seemed to almost revel in the process of eliminating her rivals with deadly force. She always made sure to send a message to her competitors, and she was undoubtedly one of the most feared, albeit unstable, drug lords of her era. In the words of Stephen Schlessinger, an attorney and the man who prosecuted her, "she was a complete sociopath. She murdered people at the drop of a hat," sometimes simply because "she didn't like the way they looked at her" (Simoni, 2018). She had begun her career initially as a petty criminal and sneakthief on the streets of Medellín. But before long, she had made a name for herself in the production, smuggling, and sale of cocaine—a highly addictive and incredibly lucrative substance refined from the coca plant, a species indigenous to much of South America. Colombia is one such country, and it was here that Griselda began her reign and her relationship with the white, powdery narcotic.

Of course, Griselda's violence was not contained within Colombia. Within a short time of entering the criminal underworld, she had expanded her cocaine empire across the Caribbean Sea to Southern Florida, New York, and later in her life, California. Everywhere she went to expand her narcotics empire, she left a trail of bloodshed behind her, starting full-blown gangland wars and executing rival smugglers *en masse*. Whatever may be said about her ultraviolent tactics, there is no doubt that they were effective. By the time Griselda's reign ended, she had become the most feared drug lord in her territory. Her main area of operations, Miami, saw a threefold increase in its homicide rate when Griselda began importing cocaine into the coastal Florida city (Preston, 1982). Bodies lined the streets as a result of her drug wars, and shootings became an everyday occurrence: shopping centers, airports, and nearly every intersection in the city could at any moment become the scene of a grand and gruesome massacre reminiscent of Chicago in the prohibition period. Many believe that Griselda deserves sole credit for turning Miami into the homicide capital of the entire United States by 1980. Of course, the infamous Pablo Escobar also contributed to Miami's reputation, but even his aggressiveness and brutality could not measure up to that of the Queenpin.

Griselda Blanco and her enterprise were not remarkable for their brutality and violence alone. What was perhaps more impressive was the massive success that she enjoyed and how vital Griselda was in the incredible boom of the cocaine industry in the United States in the 1970s and 1980s. Griselda's operation accounted for an enormous portion of the overall amount of cocaine imported into the country each year, and had evolved her smuggling methods over the years from small amounts carried on passengers via commercial flights to entire plane loads of cocaine and cannabis flown directly from Colombia into the United States. In fact, many of the running routes that she had established remained in use for decades. Griselda had flooded the streets of New York and Southern Florida with narcotics, and she profited massively as a result. Again, sources are inconsistent as to exactly how much money Griselda's cartel pulled in during her tenure, but it seems the consensus is that her revenue amounted to at least tens of millions in USD per month during the height of her business in Miami. This was more than enough to fuel her lavish lifestyle, complete with decadent parties, flashy clothing, and a severe addiction to her own drug. Without a doubt, Griselda Blanco was an obscenely wealthy woman. Since her death in 2012, she has gone down in history as the world's first female drug smuggler to become a *billionaire*. She truly was a self-made woman, in every sense of the term.

Despite her cruel legacy, it is not entirely surprising that Griselda's story is a source of inspiration for many. She was a woman who took control over an entire industry and subculture dominated by violent men. She went as high as anyone could go in the world of cocaine smuggling, where female leaders were unheard of. Proving that femininity and the use of violence were not mutually exclusive, Griselda was able to subvert and operate within a traditionally patriarchal realm. It does not take a big stretch to imagine how someone could find her legacy empowering while also denouncing her brutal tactics. Some even believe that Griselda's overuse of violence was likely a necessity for her, as she had to be able to prove herself to her male peers and establish herself as a dominating force rather than an easy target. In her line of work, being an easy target meant a very early grave.

According to Serena Simoni, the phenomenon surrounding Griselda Blanco was "one of the most advanced examples of feminization of crime" (2018). It's certainly difficult to think of another example of a woman crime lord as prominent as Griselda. In fact, the only one that is likely to come to mind is the infamous American crime duo of Bonnie and Clyde, the couple who plagued the central United States, roaming around staging daring armed robberies. But even Bonnie Parker's legacy could not come close to the success and ferocity of the Godmother, Queen of Cocaine. Given the fact that Griselda's rap sheet outshines Bonnie Parker's by a large margin, the question must be asked: Why do so few people seem to know about Griselda Blanco and her impact, whereas Bonnie is an immortalized cornerstone of criminal Americana? Much of this has to do with the overpowering legacy of Griselda's successor: the infamous Pablo Escobar, one-time friend and apprentice, and undisputed leader of the Medellín Cartel until his death in 1993.

To this day, Griselda's history remains overshadowed by Escobar, despite the fact that she outlived him. Although, modern retellings of her criminal career have steadily implanted her back into criminal mythology. Billy Corben's 2006 documentary *Cocaine Cowboys* and its 2008 sequel subtitled *Hustlin' with the Godmother,* in particular, has brought the Queenpin rolling back into the public consciousness. Just recently, in 2021, another entry into the franchise, a six-part Netflix docuseries subtitled *The Kings of Miami* was released, once again renewing the intrigue of her life. Today, despite the towering legacy of Escobar, Griselda Blanco is "one of the most mythologized drug lords in history, and certainly the most ruthless" (Brown, 2008). This is due in no small part to the simple fact that we know relatively few hard facts about her life, thus leaving plenty of room for rumors to develop into myth and legend. What we do know is that Griselda led an incredible life, revolutionized an industry, and altered the very social fabric of more than one city. Before El Chapo, there was Griselda. Before Pablo Escobar and the legendary Medellín Cartel, there was Griselda. This book will explore the life of the Godmother of

Cocaine, address the most mysterious aspects of her career, and seek to uncover exactly what turned a young girl from Cartagena, Colombia, into the most feared woman in the Americas.

Chapter 1: A Girl From Cartagena

Before we explore the details of Griselda Blanco's criminal career and fortune, we must understand where she came from. To put it mildly, the situation in which she grew up was not exactly ideal. Colombia was a nation in crisis, and there is much to suggest that her environment in these early years fundamentally influenced the woman she would become.

Humble Beginnings

In the far north of Colombia, along the shores of the Caribbean Sea, lies the beautiful coastal city of Cartagena. It is the capital and largest city in Bolívar, one of the 31 departments in Colombia. On the 15th of February 1943, it also became the birthplace of one of the most deadly crime lords in history. Today, the picturesque beach city is known for its historical richness, luxury hotels, and thriving tourism industry for wealthy vacationers. Griselda's Cartagena was wildly different. Her Cartagena was filled with Colombia's desperate poor who lived in run down makeshift huts with corrugated tin sheets for roofs. Growing up in one of the poorest neighborhoods in the city, Griselda was surrounded by violence and instability since the day she was born.

Murder was an everyday occurrence in the city in the 1940s and '50s. It was so rampant that there are stories of local children filling the holes they had dug in the earth with the dead bodies they found in the streets, just to pass the time. In fact, the extreme poverty that families in this area of Cartagena faced meant that many children themselves often had to resort to crime and petty theft just to feed themselves and help their families. It is very likely that the young Griselda Blanco had become almost completely desensitized to violence and murder before she even reached adolescence.

Griselda's home life offered no respite from the harsh outside world. Her mother was a prostitute (a common profession for women in Colombia and elsewhere living in extreme poverty) who was reportedly violent and highly unpredictable, frequently beating young Griselda as punishment (or merely as a coping mechanism for herself). To make matters worse, her stepfather had apparently been known to sexually abuse her. However, we have to again distinguish between myth and reality here. There is no doubt that Griselda had a challenging and violent upbringing; however, her childhood is the most mysterious part of her life, and very little can be taken as fact. One of Griselda's aliases was "The Black Widow," a nod to her reputation for murdering her husbands. Several accounts of her life lean into this reputation hard, drawing connections between Griselda's violence toward her husbands and her difficult childhood. It is possible that smaller details, such as the sexual abuse she suffered, may have been additions or embellishments in order to serve the overall sensational image of Griselda and her mythology. Unfortunately, we will likely never know for certain. Some sources even disagree on where she was born—while most acknowledge her birthplace of Cartagena, few others seem to suggest she was, in fact, born in Medellín. Regardless of the variations in small details, the first few years of Griselda's childhood had clearly primed her for a life of crime and viciousness, which she embraced with a distinct eagerness and unique flair.

Murder in Medellín

Cartagena was not the only city to influence Queenpin's formative years. At some point during her childhood, she and her family relocated to Medellín, Colombia's second largest city and capital of the Antioquia department. Today, Medellín holds a place in many people's minds as a lawless, crime-ridden paradise for drug smugglers and as the former headquarters of the notorious cartel leader, Pablo Escobar. When Griselda first moved to the city, however, it did not yet have this reputation. Still, it was a deeply troubled city with rampant crime, whose problems Griselda would only add to in her adulthood. Once again, the young girl was faced with surviving in an impoverished, unforgiving, and incredibly unstable environment. Griselda likely developed her toughness and ferocity during childhood as a way to simply get by her day-to-day life.

All of Colombia at the time was under threat. Around the time Griselda had left Cartagena for Medellín, the country was experiencing a period known as *La Violencia*, or The Violence. In April 1948, when Griselda was just five years old, a member of Colombia's Liberal Party and a candidate for president, Jorge Gaitán, was assassinated. His killing shook the capital city of Bogotá and resulted in an hours-long riot known as *El Bogotazo*, which claimed the lives of thousands of the city's citizens. More importantly, it kicked off a brutal civil war in Colombia between the country's Conservative and Liberal parties. The conflict lasted for a decade, and from 1948 to 1958, the country was crippled, disorganized, and in very dire straits. A majority of the fighting took place in the rural areas, but there was no part of Colombia left untouched by the violence. The breakdown of the government meant the bureaucratic functions of the cities fell into disrepair, contributing to the lack of stability everywhere Griselda went. By the end of the conflict, the fighting had taken roughly 200,000 lives of Griselda's fellow Colombians. Her situation could scarcely have been worse.

Of course, Griselda Blanco was not the only youngster to grow up in harsh conditions in one of Colombia's many slums. Today there are millions of girls just like Griselda, growing up in conditions just as brutal and desensitizing across the world. So, the question must be asked: Why don't we see thousands of Griselda Blanco's popping up every day, all over, as a result of their traumatic past? The well-known psychological concept of "nature or nurture" comes to mind. That is, does a person's environment and upbringing determine their adult personality, or is it rather due to some innate predisposition? Without a doubt, Griselda's surroundings deeply influenced her callousness. But obviously, there was something very special about her. It wasn't enough that Griselda was exposed to the horror of Medellín's streets, and it wasn't enough that she was desensitized to the carnage. She must have been drawn to it, fascinated by it. Perhaps she saw it as a powerful tool. If her later life is anything to go by, she very likely enjoyed it. Whatever the case truly is, popular media has already made up their mind about her: She was simply a psychotic, cold-blooded killer who found satisfaction in murder.

Medellín is the city where Griselda developed her taste and talent for breaking the law. Innocently enough, she began as a simple thief, lifting change and goods off pedestrians in the city streets and sideways. Still not even a teenager, Griselda proved to be quite skilled at making an illicit income. A little later in her life, she would (reportedly) follow in her mother's footsteps. She began working as a prostitute and frequently put in hours at one of Medellín's several brothels. Again, underage prostitution was not uncommon for a girl in her position, but her experiences both with her stepfather and the men she encountered during her time as a sex worker no doubt shaped her future relationships with men, which make up a large portion of the Blanco mythos. By this point in her life, there was nothing at all remarkable or shocking about Griselda's life. Pickpocketing and sex work were ubiquitous in Medellín's poorer districts. But Griselda soon took a drastic next step, and her days as a petty criminal were soon over.

In the southeastern portion of the city, east of the Medellín River and hugging the Aburrá mountain range lies *Las Manzanas de Oro*, better known as El Poblado, the upper class neighborhood of Medellín's wealthiest and most prominent. It is also the economic hub of Medellín and served as Griselda's home in her retirement years. In a region with such drastic wealth inequality, being a resident of a neighborhood with a reputation for being notoriously affluent would certainly make one a target for those whose poverty had forced them into a life of crime. One of those people, preteen Griselda Blanco, had recently fallen in with a rough crowd of other poor youths. Together, the young gang committed several crimes, including burglaries and armed theft, a notable step up from Griselda's recent criminal past. One night, Griselda and her friends descended from their poor Medellín district into the luxury of El Poblado. Looking to make a large score, they had planned something risky. The gang kidnapped a 10-year-old boy, child of a wealthy local family. Holding the boy captive in their hideout, the gang tried to extort ransom money from the family. Surprisingly, the boy's parents were unwilling to negotiate or pay anything to the young captors. The plan had failed. But certainly they couldn't just let the boy run off to expose them. As the story goes, Griselda was handed a loaded pistol and was either ordered, or dared, to kill the boy. She obliged, fatally shooting the child in the head.

So, Griselda had allegedly taken her first victim's life when she was only 11 years old. It was certainly a defining moment in her life, and while she often had others do her dirty work, she would go on to be responsible for hundreds more killings. Griselda was no longer a typical impoverished youth making a meager income off small crimes. She was now acquainted with murder and she had now proven what she was capable of, but she was not yet the Godmother, nor had she earned herself The Black Widow moniker. The world of cocaine was still a few years away for Griselda, but the two would prove to be a potent combination, especially for the cities of Medellín and Miami.

Chapter 2: A Tale of Two Cities

A significant part of Griselda Blanco's legend is, essentially, a story of two intertwined cities separated by the Caribbean Sea. Medellín and Miami, roughly 1,400 miles apart and yet became united in their years of suffering caused by Griselda Blanco and the incredible reach of her organization. In the span of just a few decades, the Queenpin's cocaine empire had left the two urban zones almost unrecognizable, with corpses overflowing their morgues and their reputation in the ground. In this chapter, before continuing Griselda's personal journey, we'll take a brief look at the landscape and history of Medellín and Miami, and how Griselda's reign of the 1970s and '80s ruptured their social life.

The City of Eternal Spring

Medellín's affectionate nickname comes from its reputation for seemingly endless springtime weather. Never too hot, never too cold, and nestled in Colombia's beautiful mountainous terrain, Medellín could have been paradise. Unfortunately, the city was facing serious problems even before Griselda turned it into a headquarters for international cocaine exporting. When Griselda was still a child, Medellín was a city of about 360,000 inhabitants, but it was already growing rapidly. This population growth was not necessarily a benefit to the old steelworking city. Many of the new migrants were refugees from Colombia's countryside and had fled to escape the terror and destabilization of *La Violencia*, which had begun a few years earlier. This meant that a majority of the new arrivals had only ever known a rural lifestyle, and life in the city was a drastic change. Almost invariably, the migrants were desperately poor, with no way to afford permanent housing in a city that was already overcrowded. Shanty towns, complete with makeshift huts, sprung up everywhere, and Medellín's slum population exploded.

Wealth and income inequality had already been serious issues in the city, with the local industrial and economic hub of El Poblado gleaming in comparison to neighborhoods filled with hovels crafted from corrugated metal. Medellín today, while in many ways a brand new city, still struggles with an economic disparity between the best and worst off. The 1950s saw the implementation of the so-called "Medellín Master Plan," a scheme to greatly expand and modernize the city. It continued through the decade but faced several problems through the 1960s, which stalled its progress. The decade also saw the continuation of significant migration into the city which, while opening new opportunities for Medellín's budding industrial districts, also led to increased population density, a lack of access to public services for poor folk, and rising unemployment as the city's factories failed to keep up with the supply of labor. Medellín was a breathtakingly beautiful city marred by the image of thousands of urban poor struggling to survive.

At least as early as the 1960s, Medellín was already home to the original criminal unit, which would morph into Pablo Escobar's infamous Medellín Cartel. This juvenile form was involved in various smuggling operations, which involved several reliable routes, and by that time, the trafficking of cannabis grown in the Colombian countryside was already an established practice. The coca plant was already known to be narcotic, but had traditionally only been cultivated by indigenous groups for various ceremonial rites and events. It was relatively recent that processed coca became a highly popular consumable and recreational drug among Colombia's population. What was missing from the equation was a large, wealthy consumer base with plenty of disposable income and a penchant for partying. Griselda Blanco would be the first to forge a connection between this ideal demographic and the source of the white powder itself. Then, Medellín's cartel would see astronomic profit growth, and the city itself would face problems like never before.

God's Waiting Room

Situated on the coast, near the extreme tip of the Florida peninsula, is the beautiful city of Miami. While Medellín clearly had numerous problems of its own well before Griselda Blanco came along, Miami was a world apart. The second biggest city in

Florida and one of the richest in the entire country, it was luxurious, prosperous, and saw a healthy (and more manageable) population increase which fueled the growth of affluence of the city. Especially after the end of the Second World War, many veterans and old folks decided to start retiring to the Sunshine State to spend their lives in one of the most naturally beautiful areas in the United States. Vast numbers of these retirees chose Miami as their ultimate destination. South Beach, a seaside Miami neighborhood, saw an especially large influx of mainly Jewish seniors. Florida, and especially Miami, was the place to be.

Before either Griselda or Escobar ever set foot in the state, Miami and Florida as a whole had already had a massive Latin American influence, and a large portion of their population had been first or second-generation immigrants from one of the many Caribbean and South American nations. Long standing cultural and economic ties also existed between the city and the Latino world. It is unsurprising, then, that in 1959, when Cuban revolutionary Fidel Castro overthrew the small island's American-friendly government, many wealthy Cubans fleeing the country for fear of retribution chose Miami as their destination of choice. Many industry owners feared that their wealth would be appropriated and their businesses nationalized, and believed that their business and familial ties in the United States would secure them a better future. Interestingly, this would not be the last large influx of Cubans from the new regime into the city of Miami, and the next one would be far more destabilizing for a city that was already embroiled in conflict.

Many of these Cuban immigrants were successful, and in fact, there had already been a small and relatively peaceful cocaine ring operating in Miami and run by Cubans in the years before Griselda revolutionized the industry and introduced a good mix of violence. For some time, Miami had a casual, manageable relationship with the narcotic powder. Generally speaking, it was used recreationally by a comparatively narrow sector of the population and was seen as an upper class drug not viable for mass consumption. Griselda's intrusion into the market, controlled largely by Cubans, is a story for later chapters, but suffice to say, this easygoing drug culture would soon erupt in spectacular fashion.

So, in the years leading up to Griselda first introducing the famous Medellín-Miami cocaine smuggling routes, Miami was a flourishing city. The city enjoyed immigration both from other American states and from the Latin American world. The Cuban situation in particular was important, as it pushed the city's demographics even further in favor of the Hispanic minority (which would eventually become the majority). It is very likely that Miami was chosen as an ideal location for the epicenter of cocaine distribution not only because of its access to the sea and its proximity to the Latin world, but because it would have been considerably easier to conduct business there. Cartel members already needed to communicate with discretion and from the vast distance between Medellín and Miami, so the ability to speak the same language with fluency would have been a great boon. Miami was a city in which the cartels could recruit locally without fear of language or cultural barriers between them and their counterparts back in Colombia.

Cocaine Wonderland

Residents of neither Medellín nor Miami understood at the time that the fates of their respective cities were soon to be deeply intertwined. Medellín had big enough problems already, and it's unlikely that the city's poor had figured that it could get much worse. Miami, on the other hand, had the look and feel of a community so idyllic and peaceful that it seemed impossible for anything to go wrong. Certainly no one expected the explosive growth of a criminal enterprise that would turn the streets into a warzone and very nearly bring the city, a haven for the nation's tired and elderly, to its knees. The 1970s and '80s would be an entirely new era for both cities.

Aside from a stint operating in New York City, whose criminal underworld at the time was monopolized by the Italian-American Mafia, Griselda's invasion of the Southern Florida market was the true start to her empire. As the cocaine and cannabis began to flow out of Medellín and into Miami, bodies began to pile up in both cities. Medellín saw a sharp rise in its already lofty homicide rate, with drug-related driveby shootings, kidnappings, and bombings becoming daily hazards. Griselda had sought to eliminate competition in her hometown in order to secure a steady supply of raw cocaine to fuel her growing empire. One particular method of murder, the flashy motorcycle driveby, was pioneered by Griselda in Medellín. It proved to be a quick, efficient means of burying rivals.

By the early 1980s, Medellín was in serious trouble and was earning its poor reputation. The city had become so dangerous that the American consulate shut its doors and ceased operation in 1981 due to security concerns arising from the daily killings and increasing brazenness of the cartel members. The narco hitmen had begun targeting more prominent people with an increase in deadly tactics, and it was clear that they were unafraid to make attempts on the lives of political figures. As a result, even the Drug Enforcement Administration (DEA) pulled out their agents from Medellín and other parts of Colombia in 1984, as the situation worsened and their lives were put in danger.

Griselda was, of course, not the only one to aid in Medellín's criminal downfall. Pablo Escobar was also a continuing source of terror for the city, even after Griselda had been taken out of the cocaine business. For some time, Escobar's cartel had great influence in the city's political scene, allowing him to essentially run his part of the city however he saw fit. The suffering continued. In 1987, for example, Medellín witnessed over 3,000 homicides that year alone (Borrell, 1988). Of course, not every murder was a direct result of Griselda and Escobar's organizations, but they certainly helped cultivate the culture of murder and lawlessness which plagued the city for decades. Even the mayor at the time, William Gomez, was forced to admit that Medellín had a serious problem with violent crime related to the narcotics trade, and even hinted that he himself was a likely target for cartel assassination.

The city's wealthier citizens would often pay for armed bodyguards to accompany them when they ventured out of their luxury homes. Police patrols carried with them high-powered assault rifles, preparing for a public shootout at any moment. Heavy weaponry was a necessity for the police just to be able to keep up with the cartels, who were generally better equipped and more well-funded than the municipal or department police force. The American cocaine market brought in so much money for Griselda and Escobar that they could easily outfit their henchmen with some of the best weapons the world had to offer, including American and Israeli-made automatic rifles and submachine guns. In the late 1980s, though the city had felt this way for years, Medellín was finally officially announced as the most dangerous city in the world.

Miami also faced unprecedented circumstances once Griselda Blanco stepped onto the scene. Beginning around 1978, when she first began establishing the smuggling routes from Medellín, Miami witnessed an abrupt upward trend in violent crime and homicide rates. Within a few years, the city was overwhelmed. Miami's infrastructure was not prepared to deal with the amount of crime and the resultant corpses that severely backlogged the city's coroner's office. There was simply no room to store the bodies, an estimated 50% of which were a direct result of gangland shootings and assassinations related to the nascent cocaine trade. Hitmen were often smuggled into the city from Colombia to carry out killings and then smuggled back to Colombia to make the job of law enforcement that much more difficult. South Florida was turning into the United States' new Wild West.

By the late 1970s, Miami's reputation was already starting to crumble. The city was no longer famous for its beaches or nightlife, its peaceful elderly communities or its impressive skyline, but rather for its toxic relationship with cocaine and murder. So much cocaine was being pumped into the city that the media virtually gave up on reporting on the seized shipments. If they ran a story on every truck, plane, or boatload of cocaine that was seized, the news would have been a simply endless torrent of the same story, with different dates.

This damaged public perception of Miami had some serious consequences for the city's demographics. A city in a state of daily unrest is the last place folks want to retire to, and the rest of the nation quickly took note of Miami's situation. Especially after 1980, the influx of elderly and newly retired Americans into Miami and South Beach took a steep decline. Eventually, it fell off altogether. On top of this, many elderly residents were moving out of the city, seeking new and safer homes elsewhere. Miami was no longer an attractive city, and by the end of the drug wars, this community had all but disappeared. Cocaine and killing sprees had turned Miami into a different city. It was still "God's Waiting Room," but its new meaning was a little more grim. By 1988, after Griselda's era of fear had ended and

Escobar had ushered in a new one, Miami was the most dangerous city in the United States of America.

Chapter 3: The Myth Begins

As we have already discussed, a significant portion of Griselda Blanco's mythology lies in her femininity and her relationship with men. Griselda had married three times over the course of her life and had taken several lovers. As the legend goes, Griselda was either directly or indirectly responsible for the murders of every one of her spouses, earning her the title "Black Widow." Here, we will take a look at the origins of this mythology and look at why it became such a fundamental part of Griselda's legacy.

Turning Tricks and Picking Pockets

One of the most defining, yet overlooked, moments of Griselda's life happened well before her introduction into the realm of cocaine. At the time, Griselda was still very young and had already been involved in miscellaneous small crimes as well as prostituting herself at a local Medellín brothel, despite the fact that until she died, she vehemently denied being involved in sex work at any point in her life. One night, while she was allegedly serving drinks and flirting with the brothel customers to try to sneak extra tips, she met a man that would soon become her first husband. His name was Darío Pestañas Trujillo (although some sources, including the notable *Cocaine Cowboys II* documentary as well as a 2021 article by Daniel Rennie, claim that the man's true first name was in fact "Carlos"). Griselda was clearly not a stranger to living outside the law, but it was Darío who first introduced the young girl to *organized* crime, as opposed to the scattered, opportunistic crime that Griselda had become accustomed to since her pre-adolescence.

Darío, years older than Griselda but still a young man himself, was no crime lord. He was simply a small-time gangster who ran his own small crew out of Medellín's slums. Although it was common for groups of kids to band together in small criminal cliques for survival in the desperately poor areas of the city, Darío's gang was hierarchical and far more organized. Griselda was likely instantly smitten by the man's lifestyle and income. Together, Griselda and Darío dealt in various crimes, including large robberies and kidnappings. It was with Darío that Griselda began to develop and harness her ferocity. Of course, she had to. She was surrounded by men who likely did not take the young girl seriously and doubted her ability to carry her own weight in such a violent criminal subculture. In order to gain the respect and acceptance of her male counterparts, Griselda had to display a certain aggressiveness and ruthlessness. As it turns out, this was quite natural for her. No doubt, the men in Darío's gang had not encountered a girl like Griselda before. Even before she became the Queenpin, she was a woman deserving of fear.

At some point during Griselda's time with the gang, she and Darío fell in love. When she was still a teenager, the couple married and continued living out their Bonnie and Clyde fantasy for some time. Over the course of the marriage, Darío had fathered the first three of Griselda's four children, all sons. Their names were Dixon, Uber, and Osvaldo Trujillo. The fourth son would be along two marriages later. Later in their lives, Griselda had introduced her sons into her cocaine business, in which they became key players. Dixon, the eldest, was especially close in his involvement in the upper workings of the empire, and would be up until the very end. Although they were important figures in the cartel, Griselda's involvement of her boys in the deadly business would come back to haunt her in later years.

So Griselda had completed her first elevation in crime. She was no longer the street urchin who had fled the abuse of her family home years before. She was no longer penniless. Griselda had finally begun to build a life for herself and, although it was firmly outside legal boundaries, it was promising and lucrative. She had a good income and was in love with a brand new family. But things would not last with Darío, who proved to be only a minor detour in the overall story of Griselda Blanco. The final chapter of her time with her first husband is when the "Black Widow" mythology finds its roots, and the details surrounding Darío's death are one of the most contested aspects of her history.

The Black Widow is Born?

Sometime in the late 1960s, the couple's marriage fell apart. Accounts differ quite a bit on exactly what happened. It seems certain that the couple had divorced at some point before Darío's death, but how he died is another question. According to some, Darío, who had been suffering from poor health issues for some time, had sudden liver failure. Griselda, who apparently still had feelings for him, desperately sought medical treatment. Eventually, Griselda desperately flew him to the United States for more expert treatment, but it was apparently no use. Darío died shortly after, and Griselda had his body shipped back to Medellín. According to this explanation, her first husband's death began a small cultural tradition in Medellín of parading the bodies of deceased loved ones through the streets in their caskets prior to the burial ceremony. These would often be accompanied by open parties in the streets and public mourning.

Another version of Darío's death is more sinister and suggests that his long criminal lifestyle eventually caught up with him. Together, Darío and Griselda had secured quite a bit of power in the local region as their operations expanded. At the time, Griselda had not yet made a big name for herself, and so Darío was assumed to be the dominant partner. Some of his associates had apparently believed that he was too powerful for his own good and that he was becoming too greedy. This story ends with Darío being gunned down outside a gas station in Colombia in the early 1970s, leaving Griselda a widow and three boys without a father.

Aside from these two accounts, the "Black Widow" mythology offers yet another explanation. According to this story, the marriage ended with Darío becoming the first husband of Griselda's to meet their end under her orders. It's unclear exactly what prompted the killing, but given what we know for sure about her life, it could have been *anything*. It could have been a serious dispute over business or profits, revenge over infidelity, or simply a minor dispute that Griselda was offended by. With someone as unpredictable as the future Queenpin, anyone's guess is perfectly plausible. All we know for sure is that Darío was dead, and Griselda was preparing to soon move on to the next phase of her monumental criminal career.

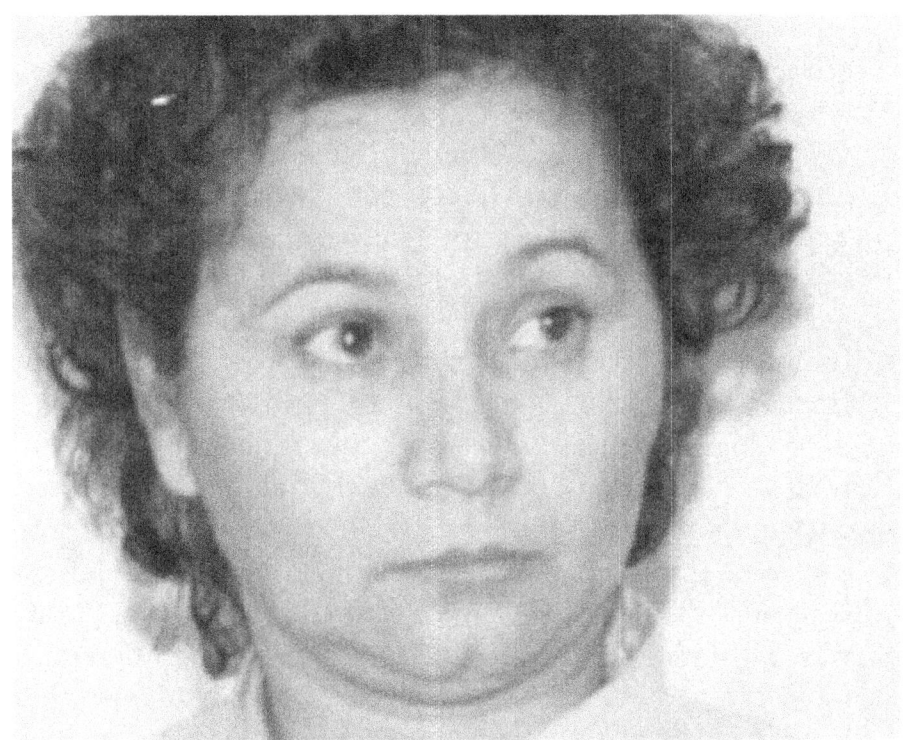

Before taking a look at Griselda's next stage of life, it is worth pausing for a while to consider why the "Black Widow" mythology dominates so much of the discussion and aura around Blanco's story. As we have seen, Griselda had a poor relationship with men since her earliest years. It would be unsurprising if the young woman, gaining more power by the day, took out her excess rage on the various men involved in her life, especially those who crossed her. According to some of the literature on Griselda, many women seem to take her story as strangely empowering. It seems that success stories of dominant women within *any* male-dominated industry, regardless of that industry's legal status, can be taken as liberating. And Griselda certainly dominated.

According to Simoni, by operating within the cocaine industry the way she did, Griselda was able to challenge the masculine (and often sexist) nature of the Colombian worlds of smuggling and narcotics, while not sacrificing her femininity. Again, the development of Griselda's aggressiveness was likely a necessity for her in order to succeed in her line of work. She could not be seen as weak by her male peers, both for safety and reputational reasons. In this way, Griselda's journey is closely reminiscent of the challenges of women in the armed forces. Female military personnel have the challenge of equaling their male counterparts in a realm that, until fairly recently, barred women from joining. Now, they often have to deal with the psychological pressure of ensuring that they are able to match what the men can do, or risk not being taken seriously or seen as a teammate on equal footing. They, like Griselda, had to prove to everyone around them that womanhood and the use of violent behavior when necessary were compatible concepts. Seen this way, Griselda's history begins to appear a bit different, a bit more sympathetic. However, of course, the first generations of women in the military were not known to go on cocaine-fuelled killing sprees and order the deaths of entire families.

According to Howard Campbell, "crime is a vehicle for liberation of a sort" (Pobutsky, 2009), and women involved in drug cartels are able to secure a sense of power and agency the more they advance within the hierarchy. Griselda's obsession with power and control over her world very likely grew out of a desire to secure a semblance of control over her life, which had been denied to her since childhood. This psychological aspect, on top of what we already know about her relationship with her second husband, likely has much to do with the gravitation toward the mythology of the husband killing, cocaine dealing badass. Without a doubt, Griselda's experience as a woman was a big part of her experience as an international drug lord. In later chapters, we will take a look at how Griselda's femininity worked in her favor on several fronts.

As the story relates to Darío Trujillo, this aspect makes it much less obvious that he was in fact murdered by, or under, the orders of, Griselda. However, the situation is far more clear in the case of her second husband, and it seems likely that much of the "Black Widow" legend is rooted in at least some fact. Griselda's husbands would universally find her difficult, especially to work with. She vexed and confused them, intimidated and overshadowed them. The men in Griselda's life could barely *understand* her, and therefore, had no hope of controlling her.

Chapter 4: Murder and White Powder

By this point in Griselda's life, she was a seasoned criminal but had not yet considered the potential windfall profits of cocaine smuggling. Darío Trujillo, her first promotion in crime, was now dead, and Griselda would soon take a new love interest in the man who would induct her into the business that eventually made her a billionaire. He would also be the man to lead Griselda into her first trouble with law enforcement, and they weren't even Colombian.

The Man From El Poblado

In the immediate aftermath of her first husband's death, Griselda was, by most accounts, still living in Medellín as a street hustler and local gangster. While there, she met another man who she quickly took a liking to, before hardly any time had passed since Trujillo's death (or murder). This new love interest's personality seems like that of an exaggerated Darío Trujillo: He was a flashy, playboy-ish hotshot from the city's wealthy El Poblado district. His name was Alberto Bravo, and he would become second husband to the future Godmother of Cocaine.

As with Darío, Griselda was likely taken in by Alberto's lifestyle and the obvious signs of wealth and status symbols. She wanted power and thus gravitated to those who clearly had it. Whether or not she truly loved these people, or simply viewed them as a means to acquire more power for herself, is not entirely clear. While she reportedly would do anything for her sons, she was not easily forgiving with her husbands, especially when she felt she wielded as much power as them.

Initially, Alberto was known to play coy with Griselda when she inquired about the source of his clearly substantial income. He admitted to running various small criminal operations, which were true, but none of them seemed to explain his lifestyle. The small businesses he told Griselda about should have given him an easy, comfortable life, not a lavish one. If Alberto wasn't hiding anything from her, he was certainly living far above his means. He eventually told Griselda that he was also involved in routine high-end robberies, which apparently provided him with substantial lump sums of cash. According to some sources, Griselda had, by this time, also established a smuggling operation of a different kind: people. Forging fake identities for South Americans wanting to enter the United States, and then providing passage for them, was lucrative for Griselda and Alberto. These smuggling routes were likely what provided the foundation for the couple's future cocaine imports. Interestingly, identity document forging and immigrant smuggling were also a widely used source of income for the Italian-American Mafia in its early years.

So, Griselda was already aware of, and involved in, many of Alberto's criminal enterprises. Still, something appeared to be missing. But before long, her second husband let her in on the secret of his real wealth, the most lucrative of his businesses: cocaine manufacturing, smuggling, and dealing. The substance was not unfamiliar to people in the region, but its use as a global cash cow was still in its immature years. Harvested and refined from two different species of South American plant into its powdered hydrochloride form, cocaine is highly addictive and has ruined many lives, and even entire cities. It's also as good as gold.

The New York Connection

Griselda took to the world of cocaine with ease. Together, she and Alberto grew the business that he had been managing for years. Typically, Alberto would purchase legal, medical grade cocaine from a Medellín clinic in as large a quantity as he could get, and then resell it on his routine trips to the U.S.A. As a united force, the couple began personally smuggling cocaine out of Colombia and into the United States, usually to New York City. Griselda's experience with forged documents helped supply her with a never-ending series of alternate identities with which to breeze past customs officials who may otherwise have questioned why the woman was so frequently in and out of the country. Usually about twice a month, the pair would make the trip stateside with cocaine strapped to themselves or hidden away in secret compartments, then sell it for a fortune to wealthy New Yorkers. Then, with their new stacks of cash, they would buy all manner of luxury goods, such as fine clothing, jewelry, and accessories from New York's finest shops to then sell back to Medellín's elite class who otherwise would have difficulty procuring such goods.

Their operation started out small, at first carrying with them only as much cocaine as she and Alberto could carry on their persons. Griselda was especially ingenious in her methods of smuggling. She had apparently enlisted the aid of a local Medellín shoemaker and repairman who would deconstruct Griselda and her husband's shoes, pack the soles with the mysterious "powder" that Griselda provided, then put the shoes back together. Those shoes would then be ripped apart and disposed of when the pair reached the United States. After all, a pair of new shoes was the least of their expenses.

Eventually, the pair started using other people as their cocaine mules; mostly women recruited and selected by Griselda. She had designed models of women's underwear outfitted with secret compartments where cocaine and cannabis could be hidden away. Griselda had apparently even opened up a small factory which produced women's clothing, some of which was dedicated specifically to the drug mules. They produced special bras and girdles for the women which could hide the cocaine and prevent it from bulging out. Roughly one full kilogram of cocaine could be strapped into one of these bras, attached to a mule, and be available for sale in Brooklyn or Manhattan in just a few hours. Each of these women could carry over $10,000 USD worth of cocaine just on their person, let alone within the compartments of their luggage.

Using women in this way was clever. Griselda understood that women were less likely to be stopped. They were less likely to appear suspicious to male customs agents and police officers. She understood that cocaine could be hidden in places on a woman that many male officers would be too hesitant or embarrassed to search or draw attention to. This special perspective gave Griselda an edge that allowed her to traffic absurd quantities of cocaine past border control and airport security, right under their noses (pun not intended). She also, allegedly, personally approved and instructed her mules. They needed to look and act a certain way, and they needed to be able to put the charm on anyone trying to stop them. They were told to always maintain a flirtatious attitude, especially when dealing with someone with any authority. Griselda knew that men could be evil, but she also knew how to expose their weaknesses.

It did not take long for Griselda's life to completely turn around. Within just the first few months of their operation in New York City, the husband and wife duo were pulling in millions. They found massive success in the states and Griselda was finally able to live the luxurious lifestyle she had been chasing since she grew up in squalor, in the shadow of the unreachable wealth of El Poblado. After a while of earning massive profits, while still based out of Medellín, the pair decided that they wanted to be a part of the American dream. Sometime in the early to mid-1970s, the two decided to move directly into their target market area, and they set up shop somewhere in the borough of Queens.

Things were good in New York, but selling cocaine wasn't a breeze. At the time, New York had its own massive criminal enterprises, and the city's narcotics industry was virtually monopolized by the infamous "Five Families" of the Italian-American Mafia. The Mafia dominated New York in those days, particularly the Genovese and Colombo Families who were both involved in the drug trade across several major American cities. Although Griselda proved efficient at dealing with and eliminating rivals, the potential combined force of the American Mafia was certainly too much for even her and Bravo to handle alone. However, whereas the Mafia had special access to the heroin market through their Old World Italian connections, who in turn had connections in opium growing regions, the Colombian smugglers had a big advantage of their own. Griselda and Bravo had direct, fresh connections to the source of refined coca. By the 1970s, the Mafia had become extensively Americanized and much of the top brass had lost their connections with Sicily. The Colombians, on the other hand, were fresh arrivals who had active connections with both the cocaine growers and smugglers. Even without a violent showdown, Griselda had wrestled and handily won a dominant share of New York City's cocaine trade from the Mafia, perhaps the biggest organized crime unit the United States had ever seen.

Although Griselda and Alberto Bravo had been profiting massively in New York, not all was well for the couple. Alberto was the one who oversaw the growing and purchasing of cocaine in Colombia, Peru, and Bolivia. Because of this, he was constantly in and out of the United States, making frequent trips back to Colombia for extended periods to ensure smooth operations and that the cocaine pipeline from the fields to the streets of New York went unimpeded. Cracks in their relationship started to form as a result of time apart, Griselda's behavior and suspicion, and disputes over money issues. Before the second half of the 1970s, their romance had broken down, and things looked like they may start to take a turn for the worse for Griselda and her new empire.

Operation Banshee

The mid-1970s, especially 1975, would be an important period for Griselda's cartel. By this time, the couple were earning millions of dollars every single month, but there were deep, underlying problems lurking behind the stacks of cash. They both took issue with the other's methods of running the business and managing their profits. Clearly, the two turned out to not be ideal partners, and Griselda would never gain a reputation for peaceful co-operation. Bravo, for his part, was certainly a dangerous man, unafraid to get his hands dirty in securing their profit. But Griselda was simply a different animal. Her ever-growing taste for violence had driven a wedge between her and her second husband. Bravo had run his smuggling operation for years without serious problems, staying under the radar and avoiding any public sensation. Griselda brought an end to all of this. No longer were the two partners of a clandestine drug operation. Now, frequent cocaine-related murders had brought them into the public eye, and Bravo and Griselda were now leaders of a murderous cartel known for their violence. As anyone familiar with the history of the Mafia, or organized crime in general will know, public attention and sensationalism are to be avoided at all cost and anonymity is key. Griselda's brutality was becoming a major problem.

The economics of Griselda's partnership were also a thorn in Bravo's side. Apparently, he had suspected Griselda for quite some time of making secret, backroom deals without Bravo's approval or even knowledge. Assuming this was an attempt to muscle in on Bravo and gain more power over him, he became defensive and paranoid. On top of this, the massive profits their operation pulled in meant little for Bravo, as their accounts were frequently being drained by Griselda. She was known to dote on her sons, the only men in her life she seemed to have an undying affection for. She would routinely withdraw massive amounts of their earnings so that she could shower her beloved sons in luxury and wealth. All this without first consulting with Alberto Bravo, her husband and business partner. To make matters worse, they both suspected the other of being unfaithful in their marriage—for good reason too, as they both likely had lovers on the side, in New York and Colombia.

In 1975, these marital and business woes were brought to a boil. Griselda had begun to lose faith in Alberto's ability to operate the Colombian side of the business. At some point, she also took note of the disappearance of millions of dollars from the couple's shared account. She immediately blamed her husband, despite the fact that she had been quite careless with their finances herself. Believing that he had either siphoned the money out to enrich himself and his own side businesses or that he had mismanaged the business so terribly as to bleed millions of dollars overnight, Griselda took it upon herself to right this wrong. She called a meeting between the two, at which they both took the time to air their grievances.

Sometime in April 1975, Griselda stepped off a plane in a Colombian airport and was escorted to the meeting with her husband. She didn't come unarmed, and she didn't come alone. The disgruntled couple met outside a trendy nightclub on the outskirts of Bogotá, each arriving with a car full of their own loyalist bodyguards. Griselda approached Alberto's car as he stepped out. He immediately blew up on Griselda. He accused her of being power hungry and allowing her newly won criminal fame and reputation as the "Cocaine Godmother" to go to her head, turning her into an egotistical megalomaniac. He criticized her for bringing so much publicity to his once-covert operation. Griselda did not take the emotional outburst well.

As the story goes, the conversation disintegrated quickly. Before long, it turned to violence. As Alberto was in the middle of chastising Griselda, the Queenpin pulled out a pistol she had concealed under her clothing. As she did, a panicked Alberto struggled to remove a silenced Uzi submachine gun he had hidden in his waistband. A gunfight between Griselda, Alberto, and their respective crews ensued. In the firefight, Griselda had been wounded in the stomach, likely by Alberto but possibly from one of his thugs. She was able to survive and escape with non-life-threatening injuries. Alberto Bravo was less lucky. Outside the nightclub, Griselda shot him several times, one of them he took directly in the face. Alberto, a man with whom Griselda had bore no children, was dead and his crew either surrendered or were also killed. Griselda was now the unquestioned leader of the cartel dominating the Medellín-New York City connection.

This story of Griselda and Alberto's showdown is certainly one of the most dramatic of her mythos and also seems to be one of the closest to reality. But, while Griselda almost certainly was responsible for her second husband's death, some sources suggest that the details of the epic, spaghetti western-style showdown between the husband and wife may have been a little embellished or exaggerated. Regardless of whether Griselda personally fired the shot that ultimately killed Alberto, or had simply ordered one of her many goons to do it, it was enough to spawn the legend of the husband-killing psychopath. Indeed, although Darío Trujillo is the first chronological instance of mariticide in her legend, it was almost certainly the story of her shootout with Alberto Bravo that turned her relationship with men into the focal point of her life legacy. The speculation that Darío was also murdered by Griselda could very well have been an addition to her story after the fact. Especially considering the fact that the vast majority of recorded accounts of Griselda's story come from well after this period of her life, this is certainly plausible. In any case, by the time Alberto Bravo was killed, the duo had built an empire that spanned two continents, employed nearly 2,000 coke dealers in the United States, and was moving hundreds of kilograms into the country on a regular basis. Griselda was now in sole control of the whole thing.

Alberto Bravo's demise was not the only monumental moment for Griselda in 1975. By this time, law enforcement had already been aware of Griselda for quite some time. Unbeknownst to her, both the New York Police Department (NYPD) and the Drug Enforcement Administration (DEA) had been investigating her and her cocaine ring for years. The two agencies had combined forces in response to the flood of cocaine in New York City, as well as to the realization that the American Mafia were no longer the only players in town. They were the team behind what was known as "Operation Banshee." It was a massive, years-long effort to investigate the drug pipeline between Colombia and the United States as well as to identify and indict the key players located in the U.S. It also happened to coincide with the renewed crackdown on organized crime in general in the U.S., which also severely affected the Mafia at the time. This was the era of indictments under the Racketeer Influenced and Corrupt Organizations Act, better known as the RICO Act of 1970. It enabled courts to prosecute individuals who were only tangentially related to a certain criminal act which had been committed in service of a broader criminal organization. This applied to Mafia-style groups as much as it did cartels. And it was a drug smuggler's worst nightmare.

In April 1975, Griselda was indicted on federal drug trafficking charges as a result of the investigations under Operation Banshee. Apparently, the indictment was triggered by the interception and seizure of a large shipment of 150 kilograms of cocaine from Colombia coming into the country. Operation Banshee had been able to connect Griselda to the shipment and began to move against the Godmother. The NYPD and DEA, however, ran into serious problems in the process. Griselda Blanco, the mastermind multi-millionaire behind the flood of cocaine, was nowhere to be found, and the law enforcement agencies that had committed countless man hours to the investigation were stymied. Many members of the American Mafia were known to flee to their ancestral Italian homes, whether in Sicily, Naples, or elsewhere. The Genovese Family, for instance, had a history of bosses and underlings who had fled to the old country, including the famous Lucky Luciano, Giuseppe Morello, and Vito Genovese himself. Griselda took a page from their book. Alert to the fact that law enforcement was hot on her trail, Griselda went on the lam and fled back to her home country of Colombia to lie low.

For now, Griselda had eluded law enforcement and once again evaded the consequences of her actions. It is possible that the fact that she was a woman allowed her to operate for so long in New York before anything manifested in the investigation, and was the reason why she had so much wiggle room to flee before she was brought before a court to face a sentence. If so, this is one of the earliest major instances of Griselda's womanhood working to her advantage. During the years that Operation Banshee was underway, it has been reported that several agents who had committed themselves to the operation experienced great difficulty in conveying the importance of Griselda herself. Many of their superiors had difficulty accepting the fact that a woman was a key player in the highest echelon of the drug trade. It was unusual and certainly unheard of for a woman to be in control of an organization like this, and some were hesitant to prosecute Griselda while an even more powerful man may still be operating from behind the curtain. Being a Queenpin, instead of a Kingpin, was proving to be a boon for Griselda.

Although she had escaped the law for the time being, federal agents had clearly caught on to Griselda's business. Before long, the higher ups in charge of the narcotics investigation would accept the fact that Griselda Blanco was a force to be reckoned with, and that it was in fact her who had been behind the mass importation of the drug directly from Colombia. Griselda was already on her way to her legacy being immortalized within American criminal culture, but her story was only just beginning by the time she fled from the state of New York. Her villainy and sheer brutality were becoming a part of the collective consciousness, especially as the so-called War on Drugs raged on throughout the United States and moral panics over the rise of drug use dominated American media. To law enforcement,

Griselda seemed like an especially unsavory character. She had no regard for civilian casualties in the course of her violence. She seemed to have no morally redeeming qualities, and the judge overseeing her case in New York even lambasted her for involving her children in her criminal activity from a young age. On top of all of this, Griselda was an immigrant from South America, fueling bigotry over migrants to the United States and providing ammunition for those claiming that immigrants brought crime. Certainly, Griselda was as reviled outside the criminal world as she was revered within it.

And so, Griselda's days of operating out of New York City were at an end. Her business there would continue for some years, however, it would ultimately become a sideshow for her, as her real fortune would be accumulated elsewhere after she was able to re-enter the American market. Well before Pablo Escobar stepped into the spotlight, Griselda was already on the main stage, at least as far as certain members of the DEA were concerned. She was there when the very first connections were established between the Colombian coca growers/cocaine manufacturers and American leaders and street dealers. She was not just one of the first *female* Colombians to smuggle mass amounts of cocaine and other narcotics into the U.S.; she was one of the first Colombians to ever do it, period. And as we've seen, if anything, it was her femininity that allowed her to prosper for so long. This enabled her to blaze a trail for those who would come later, especially Escobar, who would go on to utilize many of the smuggling routes and methods that Griselda had created and pioneered years prior.

Chapter 5: Miami's Vice

While some sources seem to suggest that Griselda had fled directly to Miami once she had been forced to flee New York State, she almost certainly first fled to Colombia and returned to the United States a few years later. During this time, however, she had not slowed down her business and was already actively moving cocaine into Miami and the ports of Southern Florida. It was no accident that Griselda's eventual permanent relocation to Miami coincided with the city's dramatic downturn. Griselda, as it turns out, was Miami's real vice.

Rule #2, Husband #3

Before Griselda found herself on her new stomping grounds in Miami, big things were already happening while she was in her self-imposed exile in Medellín. In fact, she was apparently already scheming something barely a year after she left New York. Sometime in 1976, the Colombian government had planned to send the tall ship *Gloria* to the harbors of Florida to celebrate and commemorate the United States' bicentennial anniversary of their independence, which they had won from Britain in 1776. Griselda saw an opportunity. Apparently, the plan was to load large amounts of cocaine onto the ship before it departed from Colombian shores, and then have Griselda's goons in Miami secretly offload the cargo while the *Gloria* was docked in Florida. In a way, the scheme was brilliant. The *Gloria* was a diplomatic envoy sent to celebrate the United States—for the American government to have seized and searched the ship, suspecting it of carrying illegal narcotics, would have been a huge diplomatic faux pas. However, the problems Griselda faced were logistical, and it's unclear whether or not her grand scheme ended up bearing fruit. It didn't matter, anyway. In the coming years, border control and customs would become so overwhelmed by incoming cocaine shipments that the occasional seized cargo would be nothing but a minor annoyance to Griselda.

Also in 1976, Griselda had been growing her ranks and inducting newer narcos into her operation. Perhaps she was gearing up to take Miami by storm. A young man who came to be known simply as El Mono (literally meaning "the monkey," but in Colombia the phrase is often used to refer to people with noticeably blonde hair), was one of the key hitmen recruited into Griselda's cartel. Only 17 years old at the time, El Mono, along with many other henchmen, would soon wreak havoc upon Miami in service of Griselda's quest for wealth and power. By this time, Griselda had also been employing another young hitman by the name of Jorge Ayala, better known by his nickname, Rivi. Rivi would arguably end up becoming Griselda's most trusted advisor and hitman, and the young man would rise through her cartel's ranks with ease as he led the carnage and bloodshed in south Florida. Griselda's most noteworthy young inductee, however, would not fully enter the picture until her permanent move to Miami. Soon, the Kingpin and Queenpin's criminal paths would cross.

By the late 1970s, Griselda's move to Miami was complete, and she was flooding the city more than ever before. Unfortunately for the people of Miami, Griselda was also becoming more dangerous. Some time ago, Griselda had committed one of the worst mistakes a person in her position could make. In 1983's *Scarface*, a film about Cuban cocaine smugglers in 1980s Miami, the inexperienced protagonist Tony Montana is told by his superior that the number two rule, the second most important thing to remember for a narco, is to never get high on your own supply. In other words: Sell, don't use. Tony did not heed this advice, which ultimately led to his downfall. Griselda was, by this time, not simply getting high on her own supply, but she was thoroughly addicted to it. Over time, her dependence became worse and, like Tony, the cocaine-induced paranoia was beginning to make her erratic and seriously affect her decision-making. As history has shown us, paranoia can cripple organizations, especially illicit ones like drug trafficking. The Mafia experienced this: In the 1980s, boss of the Genovese Family, Vincent "The Chin" Gigante was known as the "oddfather," noted for his extreme paranoia and fits of mania. His obsessive and compulsive secrecy and fear of leaving his home made the smooth functioning of the family virtually impossible. It seemed possible that this is what the future held for Griselda's operation, as well.

If Griselda was wild and unpredictable earlier in her life, these traits were in overdrive by the time she took control of Miami. By the middle of the 1980s, her addiction was also beginning to take a serious toll on her body. According to some sources, Griselda's preferred method of consumption was called "basuco," another name for the raw cocaine paste which must be scraped off the bottoms of barrels after the production process is complete. It's incredibly potent and even more addictive, typically smoked, and known to cause extreme paranoia. Griselda had never had much self-control over her impulses, and it's likely that this habit cost her a fortune over the years. If this indeed was what Griselda was ingesting in large quantities for years, it is a miracle that she lived to the age that she did.

Sometime in 1978, just three years after she had fatally shot her second husband, Alberto Bravo, Griselda met and soon married a man named Darío Sepúlveda. It was her third and final marriage, but he would certainly not be her last lover. Later that same year, Griselda gave birth to her fourth child, the only one not fathered by Trujillo. By this point, Griselda had fully embraced the gangster lifestyle and was enamored by pop culture gangster films. *The Godfather* was a particular favorite of hers. So, Griselda named her fourth child Michael Corleone Blanco, in honor of the film and of Al Pacino's famous character, perhaps the most recognizable Mafia figure in all of fiction. Funnily enough, the film's Michael Corleone was the youngest son to the Godfather. Apparently Griselda thought that the Godmother should have a little Michael of her own.

Although not all of his half-siblings have been as lucky, Michael Corleone survives to this day. He was, for much of his life, also involved in the so-called "cartel lifestyle," but apparently abandoned his criminal life after his mother's passing. Fortunately, however, Michael Corleone has since been very open about his and his mother's history and criminal careers. He is one of the best sources in literature for personal and intimate details of his mother's cocaine operation, and is as open about her evil deeds as he is about her nevertheless warm hearted nature. One of the other key sources, a future lover of hers, will feature prominently in the last few years of her criminal career. We will be meeting him later in Chapter 6.

So, by the late 70s, Griselda had yet another new husband, a new baby boy, a severe addiction to cocaine, and a seemingly ever-growing aggressiveness. She also had hundreds of millions of dollars to finance cartel wars and the mass assassination of her competition. If Griselda's business was booming in New York City, it was about to explode in Miami. This was the start of the downfall of Southern Florida.

Cocaine Cowboys and Escobar's Cartel

If Griselda was relatively unknown in the public eye prior to her move to Miami, she would gain a considerable reputation for herself soon, especially after 1979, when city officials began seeing the writing on the wall: Miami was in for serious trouble. Her "callous and brutal decision-making" (Simoni, 2018) proved to be a major concern for both local and federal law enforcement. As mentioned earlier, cocaine was not a new import to the city. A relatively lax drug culture had existed for years there, but Griselda's leadership completely changed the landscape of the industry. Small, clandestine deals turned into massive exchanges of kilograms of cocaine at a time. More Miamians than ever were, in one way or another, directly involved in the cocaine trade. The attitude of relatively peaceful co-operation within the cocaine industry was no more, and Griselda looked to make herself the only player in town. The killings were indiscriminate as the Godmother turned "this cocaine funland into a rollercoaster of wanton violence" (Pobutsky, 2020).

The Cubans were her first enemies upon setting up shop for good in Miami. The Cuban cocaine network had already been set up and profitable for years, and while there was clearly a large enough demand in south Florida to accommodate the two Latin American factions, Griselda was no longer willing to share the profits as she was forced to with the American Mafia in New York City. What ensued was a bona fide killing spree. Together with Jorge "Rivi" Ayala, her executioner-in-chief, as well as El Mono, the Colombian Cartel massacred the competition. Their tactics were vicious and over-the-top, and it's alleged that when Griselda ordered a hit, she intended for each one to send a message. When the hit squad entered a target's home, they didn't just kill them—they were instructed to kill everyone in the place, including women and children. Opposing Griselda not only put one's life in danger, but the lives of their wife and kids too. There seemed to be no moral compass, no code of honor whatsoever, that bound the Colombian cocaine narcos.

In very short order, the Cuban faction of the cartels had been seriously damaged as the Colombians, led by Griselda, muscled in on their territory with lethal force. In one scene in the film

Scarface, Cuban narco Tony Montana gets visibly irritated at having to conduct business with the Colombians, who he unreservedly admits to hating. The meeting itself ends in violence between the two factions. True to life, these scenes were based on the animosity and bitterness that was cultivated between the two Latino groups as a result of Griselda's drug wars. Interestingly, while Griselda herself seemed to be deeply influenced by old-time gangster films as well as *The Godfather*, the violence of *Scarface* was only able to exist due to the Miami that Griselda had created. Although her campaign against Cuban smugglers was largely successful, high-profile Cuban dealers would remain on the scene in south Florida well into the 1990s. In particular, the Americanized Cuban-born partnership of Augusto "Willy" Falcon and Salvador Magluta was able to find success even after Griselda had been taken out of the equation. For the Cubans, however, the process was far more difficult as they still relied on cocaine sourced from Colombia, the home territory of the Medellín Cartel.

The year 1979 is one of the most important in constructing the timeline of Griselda's entry into Miami. According to many, this was the most important turning point for Miami's descent into cocaine-fuelled killing sprees. After this time, a flood of media articles would fear-monger over the rise in the city's crime rate and express serious concern over the amount of drugs being seized on a daily basis coming in from South America. No longer could the police and residents of the city put their blinders on and pretend that all was well in Miami, and the media now acknowledged that the city was in the midst of a genuine drug war. And it all started in a shopping mall.

The 11th of July, 1979, was a typically hot day in Miami. It was a Wednesday, and many who weren't at work in the afternoon were shopping and seeking refuge from Florida's summer heat in the enclosed Dadeland Shopping Mall in Kendall, a borough of the biggest city in the Miami-Dade county. The mall had been a hotspot for locals ever since it was built in the 1960s and had doubled in size, since it was a place Miamians were familiar with and comfortable in. Until Griselda's drug cartel turned the mall into the scene of one of the most dramatic shootings of the decade.

Early in the afternoon of that day, two men were shopping together at Crown Liquors, one of the many shops in Dadeland Mall. Perhaps looking for a nice, expensive bottle of whiskey, there was no doubt that the two could afford it. They were both big players in Miami's exploding cocaine market, and both were Colombian. Unfortunately for them, however, they were not allied with Griselda Blanco. The men were 37-year-old German Jiminez Panesso and his associate and bodyguard, Juan Carlos Hernandez, who was all of 22 years old at the time. Earlier in the 1970s, Griselda and Panesso were amicable partners and the vast majority of Panesso's supply of cocaine was provided by the Godmother's Medellín Cartel. Apparently, in 1978, however, the relationship had soured. Sometime in the spring of that year, Panesso's home was burglarized, apparently by another member of a group linked to Griselda. Dozens of kilos of cocaine were stolen, as well as roughly a half million in USD cash. A member of his house staff was also murdered in the raid. Panesso, who by 1979 had apparently been working for another drug lord named Conrado Valencia Zalgado, better known as "El Loco," retaliated by murdering the mastermind behind the plot. Soon after, the two factions began going at each other's throats in a series of retaliatory hits. Eventually, it had to come to an end. Carlos Ramirez, the partner of the man who robbed Panesso, decided to appeal to a higher authority. He pleaded for Griselda to help him "solve" the situation with Panesso. Griselda didn't have much reason to get involved—regardless of who won, she would still be supplying just as much cocaine to the victor. But

Griselda just so happened to owe roughly one milliondollars to Panesso. She saw this as an opportunity to earn some goodwill with a favor to Ramirez while also wiping out an annoyance and a big chunk of her personal debt. Griselda agreed to take care of the little problem.

At around 2:30 in the afternoon, as the Colombian pair were picking out their alcohol, a van pulled into the Dadeland parking garage. It was apparently a commercial vehicle, with the lettering on the side reading "Happy Time Complete Party Supply." But the men who got out did not seem like the happy type, and they were there to conduct business; a bit more serious than supplying birthday parties. The driver and two passengers quickly hopped out of the parked Ford Econoline van and made a beeline for Crown Liquors. They seemed like they were on a mission, and more worrying, it seemed like they were hiding something under their shirts.

The trio approached the store where Panesso and his bodyguard were getting ready to pay for their liquor. Before they could, the three men each removed an automatic submachine gun that they had hidden under their clothing. They opened fire on the pair of narcos in broad daylight, in front of countless onlookers and witnesses. In the end, Panesso and Hernandez died in the Wild West-style shootout after exchanging fire with the assassins. Several innocent bystanders, employees of the liquor store, were also wounded in the attack, something that would become a recurring theme in cartel-related gang shootings. Afterwards, it was determined that the three men were sent by Griselda Blanco, and according to some sources, two of the men that carried out this assignment were Jorge Ayala and Miguel Sepúlveda. The latter of these men was Griselda's brother-in-law, the brother of her husband at the time, Darío Sepúlveda. These narcos earned themselves the nickname

"Cocaine Cowboys," serving as the namesake for the series of documentaries about Miami's drug wars in the mid-2000s.

After the dramatic showdown and Panesso was confirmed to be dead, the trio of Griselda's men hastily fled the scene. Initially, the crew took off in the same Ford van they had arrived in, but abandoned it at the end of the parking garage, either escaping from that point by foot or in a separate getaway car. It is a good thing that the van was left behind for police to investigate in the aftermath, because it shed much-needed light and gave law enforcement an idea of what they were going to be up against. What they found inside the van was just as shocking as the shooting itself. In the back and under the seats of what police on the scene later described as a "war wagon" were dozens of firearms including high-caliber handguns, shotguns, and fully automatic American and Israeli-made submachine guns, as well as several bulletproof vests. More than this, the sides of the van were coated in quarter inch thick steel to protect from incoming enemy fire, and cut into the doors were long, thin port holes to allow those in the interior to fire outside. It was a vehicle specially customized for gunfights and driveby shootings.

Needless to say, the contents of the van were unsettling to many on the Miami police force. They were dealing with an organization that was incredibly well-funded and equipped, moreso even than the police department, whose officers at the time were still only issued basic six-shot revolver handguns. If a shooting like this were to occur between Miami PD officers and Griselda's paramilitary troops, the police simply wouldn't stand a chance. On top of this, the van was expensive and just purchased recently, reportedly with barely 100 miles in the odometer. The fact that the men were willing to abandon a brand new, heavily customized vehicle filled with tens of thousands of dollars worth of firearms, ammunition, and vests, is a testament to how much money the cartel was bringing in, and how little they needed to worry about material expenses and funding (an issue which was very real for the unprepared Miami police department). The cartel most likely recuperated the cost of the van and all of its contents before the end of the day.

Perhaps the most disconcerting aspect of what came to be known as the Dadeland Mall Massacre was the time and location. In the middle of broad daylight in a crowded public area, Griselda and her crew were unafraid to start a firefight. The shooting almost certainly would not have made such an impact on the public psyche, nor would it have garnered the media attention that it did, if it had occurred in a dark alley at night in one of Miami's seedier neighborhoods, as had traditionally been the norm before Griselda. The Godmother was becoming more brazen and less afraid of the consequences of her actions. This was a sign of the times, as public, highly visible shootouts would become more and more common occurrences in the city streets. On the 40th anniversary of the massacre at Dadeland, Nelson Andreu, who was a detective in Miami's homicide division at the height of the drug wars, recalled how significant a realization this was for Miami: "If they want to hit or kill someone, doesn't matter where it happens, who else is around or the time of day that it happens, they're gonna get their target and everyone else better be careful and be aware of their surroundings," (Hamacher, 2019).

Although Dadeland was a significant pivotal moment for Miami and the cartels, it was simply a part of a growing trend in the area since Griselda's entrance. The months preceding Dadeland in 1979 were already the deadliest on Miami's record, and Dadeland forced many people to realize that it was only going to get worse in the coming years as the cocaine operations expanded. The city's residents were beginning to take note of the situation they were now in. As Miami's elderly residents fled the city in droves, the ones who remained behind cleaned out

Miami's gun stores. More Miamians were purchasing firearms for personal protection than ever before, understanding that their homes were no longer safe and that at any moment while out and about in the city, they could end up in the middle of a Wild West gangland shootout. Numbers of homes equipped with security systems and alarms increased, and more families began adopting trained dogs for home protection. There had also been reports of civilian vehicles being customized with bulletproof glass and steel doors, as shootings in the middle of traffic and at stop lights were not uncommon. Miami was a warzone.

Things were looking no better for the city after the turn of the decade. In fact, the first few years of the 1980s were even more foreboding, as new cocaine pushers were popping up trying to make their fortune while Griselda and the Medellín Cartel violently tried to suppress them. Narcotics continued to pour in through the Medellín pipeline, and in the first year of that decade, nearly three quarters of the total amount of cocaine being imported annually into the country was being funneled directly through south Florida ports. Also in 1980, yet another large migration from Cuba into Florida took place; however, this wave would be more problematic and far more consequential. These immigrants were not (mostly) wealthy political refugees who sought to continue their lives and businesses in the aftermath of the socialist-leaning Cuban Revolution. These were criminals, many of them violent, who had been emptied from Cuban prisons in Havana and other cities on the island.

Engraved on a bronze metal plaque at the base of New York's Statue of Liberty are the famous words which defined America's supposedly warm embrace of immigrants: "Give me your tired, your poor, your huddled masses yearning to breathe free, the wretched refuse of your teeming shore." In 1980, Fidel Castro, leader of Cuba since 1959, decided to call the United States on their bluff. In an attempt to clear out the nation's prisons (and possibly as a way to frustrate their American enemies), the Castro regime released vast numbers of violent criminals and psychiatric patients with the intent of shipping them off to the U.S. The government had already announced that they were going to allow all Cubans who wanted to leave the country to emigrate to America, claiming that the revolution did not need them, anyway. Castro had sent well over 100,000 Cubans in total to the shores of the U.S. in that year. Hidden among them were a large but unknown number of hardened criminals fresh from prison.

This fiasco had big implications for the country, and especially Miami, the city which was most flooded by the wave of arrivals from Cuba. The already overwhelmed bureaucracy now had even more work as they attempted to sort through the refugees to determine which were truly seeking asylum and which were the violent outcasts from Castro's jails. Miami officials feared the prospect of the city being inundated with new sources of crime and yet more fuel to the fire that was the Latin American cartel wars. Indeed, many of the Cuban criminals who found their way to Miami aboard one of the many refugee ships quickly ended up involving themselves in the cocaine trade, the most lucrative industry for criminals looking to make it big. The result was an increase in factional, drug-related violence and murders, as the Cuban cartels gained a fresh potential source of new narco inductees. This saga of Cuban criminal refugees was so impactful that it, in fact, served as the basis for the plot of *Scarface*, where Pacino's Tony Montana is one of the criminals sent to the shores of Florida, where he quickly climbs the narco totem pole in Miami. The resulting violence was not limited to the cartels, but Miamian society as a whole. The boom in the Cuban population resulted in more interracial tension between the Black and Latin American communities, two sectors of the city's underclass demographic who had long been competing for scarce economic resources.

Of course, not everyone entirely suffered as a result of the chaos and bloodshed that Griselda Blanco had helped plunge the city of Miami into. Despite everything, this state of affairs was a windfall for reporters and the media. Taking every opportunity to report on and sensationalize the dramatic shootings and crime scenes, which seemed to be occurring on a daily basis, it was open season for journalists just as much as it was open season for hitmen. Whereas reporters had essentially given up on reporting the non-stop stream of stories of drug busts and seizures, public shootouts in broad daylight, reminiscent of the lawless Dodge City, were simply never boring. Readers were eager to hear about the next explosive story coming out of the cocaine capital of America, whether they were the concerned and fearful folks living in Miami, or the countless others throughout the U.S. who were intrigued and scandalized by the antics of Griselda's cartel.

Indeed, Miami was becoming a nation-wide point of conversation. News outlets in other big cities were beginning to pick up on the notoriety that Miami was gaining, and the shocking and bizarre killings were fodder for journalists from all over. One such example, which would almost be humorous if it were not so morbid, involved the murder of one of Griselda's rivals in the middle of a busy Miami airport. Apparently, the drug lord was just stepping off of his plane when he was approached and stabbed to death by one of Griselda's hitmen with an actual bayonet, a blade meant to be fixed on the barrel of a gun, popularly used during the Second World War. The *Los Angeles Times* had much to say about Miami's surge in open brutality, criticizing the drug trade which had become "out of hand, with gangs of dealers... routinely shooting each other in south Florida" (Nylan, 1981). Both local and national news organizations ran similar stories throughout the early 1980s, by which time Miami's reputation was already in tatters.

In fact, the media storm that surrounded Miami very likely only made the situation worse for the residents themselves. People were paranoid, and more Miamians than ever were armed, whether they were a criminal or civilian. Much of the general paranoia had to do with the constant reminders in the news about the peril that the city was in. Some argued at the time that at least some of the fear Miamians had was unwarranted. William Wilbanks, at the time a professor of criminal justice at Florida International University, believed that the media's sensationalism greatly blew the situation out of proportion. In a 1984 paper that he wrote for the university, Wilbanks attempted to place Miami's situation within its historical context. He looked at homicide statistics in the Dade County area going back as far as 1917, and his controversial conclusion was that, in fact, the homicide rate that Miami was seeing was perhaps only *slightly* above what we might have expected to see, especially when compared with that of other large, crime-ridden cities, such as New York City and Chicago. Needless to say, this was an unpopular opinion at the time, especially among those directly affected by the violence.

Despite what Wilbanks concluded based on the historical trajectory he drew, life was palpably different in Miami. There was also no doubt whatsoever that the behavior and tactics of Griselda were becoming more spectacular and deadly. Motorcycle drivebys, the method of murder that the Godmother pioneered in Medellín and later exported to the United States, was wreaking havoc on her enemies in Miami, and spectators across the country couldn't help but take note of the undeniably slick and flashy style of public execution. Besides this, the facts on the ground speak for themselves: Reportedly, in the early years of the 1980s, an upward of a quarter of all corpses in

Miami morgues, at any given time, were suspected of being a direct result of cartel violence. The bodies all had one thing in common: They were absolutely riddled with automatic bullet holes. The Miami coroner's office admitted to having to lease large, commercial refrigerated trucks from a local fast-food chain in order to store the long list of backlogged corpses awaiting processing. Yes, things were different in Miami.

She was also causing trouble back home in Colombia, and Medellín was seeing even more cartel related violence than Miami. One particular story of a party she hosted while in Colombia gives us a glimpse of both her growing aggressiveness and increasingly erratic behavior. Sometime between around 1980 and 1982, Griselda held a large, luxurious party at her massive ranch property in San Cristóbal, a town roughly 10 kilometers from her home base of Medellín. The house was filled with guests who were all handsomely provided for by Griselda's staff. But for Griselda, the purpose of her lavish shindig was not solely to entertain her friends or to share her immense wealth. She had used the party to lure four of her underlings, who she had suspected of being government informants, and gather them in one place. In the middle of the party, as her guests were drinking and reveling and whoring, she had the four suspected rats dragged away and executed. Any shocked onlookers were reprimanded by Griselda, who demanded that they get back to the party. After all, she told them, nothing at all had happened.

Further, in both Miami and Medellín, Griselda was gaining a reputation for flying off the handle for almost any reason. Apparently, she had started more than one full-scale gang war over the slightest of insults toward any of her sons, most of whom were also involved in the cocaine trade by this point. It seems that the Black Widow did indeed have some men in her life that she cared for, and she was willing to murder anyone on their behalf, even if it was unnecessary. So, while it is likely that some of Miami's reputation may have been exaggerated as a result of exploitative news pieces on the drug trade, the fact is that the Queen of the city at the time, the woman who controlled much of the criminal underworld, was bloodthirsty, unconcerned with civilian casualties, and severely unstable.

As dangerous as Griselda was, she was no longer the only big Colombian cocaine player in the country. The legendary Pablo Escobar, the man who would come to dominate the Medellín Cartel, was now also on the scene. The two drug lords were not unfamiliar with each other; however, the information regarding their relationship is spotty at best. The pair most likely met sometime in the early 1970s, before Escobar had entered the cocaine trade. At the time, although he did run a fairly large chop shop operation, he was still just a low-tier carjacker in comparison to Griselda. Some accounts claim that Griselda was the one who introduced Escobar to the cocaine trade, which would make him obscenely rich by the 1980s, and also served as his mentor and close friend. He was even known to frequently attend many of Griselda's famous parties at her luxurious Miami Beach home. Others argue that the two were actually bitter enemies operating rival crews. It is very likely that both of these are true at the same time, and that the pair were amicable at first, but grew to compete with each other as the younger upstart Escobar's ambition began to grow, even exceeding that of the Godmother. Of course, Griselda was not known to suffer any rivals and to move aggressively on those who threatened her territory. It's also been suggested that the two had begun a romantic relationship early on, which would be entirely unsurprising given Griselda's history of taking younger lovers. Before the late 1970s, to use a Mafia term, Griselda was the "boss of bosses," while Pablo was still a young go-getter looking to seize more power and make a name for himself.

Regardless of their past relationship, Escobar was soon to become a household name. He had begun his own criminal career in the latter half of the 1960s, years after Griselda. Like her, Escobar was raised in Medellín after moving there from his birth city of Rionegro. He also was greatly responsible for aiding Griselda in making Medellín one of the most dangerous places on earth and destroying Colombia's reputation. By the late 1970s, Escobar was already importing large quantities of narcotics into the United States—including Florida, California, and Puerto Rico—and was amassing a personal fortune to rival that of Griselda's. Even with himself and Griselda flooding the country with cocaine, the demand throughout the big cities continued to rise. Escobar was also ruthless and, more importantly, his Medellín cartel held massive political influence in Colombia, allowing him to operate more smoothly (although Griselda ended up having better luck overall in evading the police). When his political clout was not enough, he was known to bribe legal officials, like judges, and when that was unsuccessful, he was not below political assassinations. Griselda's master plan to escape when she was eventually imprisoned, though it did not come to fruition, was even more spectacular than this.

Such was the state of the city of Miami during the late 1970s and early 1980s under Griselda Blanco, and Escobar would continue her legacy for years after she was gone. A skyrocketing homicide rate year-over-year, dramatic motorcycle-mounted public shootings, and a bigger market for addictive narcotics than ever before. The number of murders that Griselda was responsible for ordering numbered at least in the hundreds, and some estimates suggest the total was in fact in the thousands (Rennie, 2021). Customs agents were as overwhelmed with incoming shipments of cocaine as medical workers were with the corpses of dealers. Anyone looking with clear eyes at the state of the city in Miami knew something had to give. So did law enforcement. When Griselda fled New York in the 1970s, federal agencies did not simply forget that she existed, and, in fact, had been working to gather more information and evidence on her for some time. By around the mid-1980s, they were very much on her trail, and were beginning to close in.

Chapter 6: The Crusade

Together, Griselda and Pablo brought chaos and murder to more than one city during their times atop the cocaine underworld. Both of them were earning enough to become billionaires while still affording to be able to pay their workers handsomely, particularly in Escobar's case. The prosperity would continue for some years, but, at least for Griselda, trouble would soon be coming in two major ways: both personally and professionally.

Running From the Law

The first major problem for her had nothing to do with the law, but everything to do with cocaine. Griselda's marriage with her third partner, Darío Sepúlveda, was on the rocks. Her severe cocaine addiction was exaggerating her already frenzied behavior as well as her paranoia, and it seems that Sepúlveda was beginning to fear that she may be putting his life, as well as the life of their young son Michael, in serious danger. Griselda was not known to be merciful toward the children of her victims, so why should her enemies show any restraint with her family? Eventually, their disagreements and her unstable personality became too much for Sepúlveda to deal with. In 1983, Sepúlveda suddenly walked out of his marriage with Griselda.

Normally, this would have been no major issue for Griselda, who did not have an excellent record with her husbands in the first place. It is unclear whether Sepúlveda was aware of Griselda's reputation with her previous two husbands, but regardless, it was a brave move to potentially earn the scorn of the Godmother. But, as petty as she was, she may not have bothered to expend the time and money on taking revenge on Sepúlveda, if not for one thing: Sepúlveda had taken his and Griselda's young son Michael Corleone with him. With the boy, he had fled their Miami home on their way back to their home country of Colombia. She was incensed. Stealing away the person that Griselda perhaps loved most in the world was certainly enough to pull her attention away from her empire. She was determined to get her beloved son back and allegedly paid a massive bounty contract to have Sepúlveda tracked down and murdered in Colombia and to have Michael returned to her in Miami. It did not take long for her people to track her husband and son down. Allegedly, Sepúlveda was shot dead in the street in Colombia as Michael looked on. With Michael back with his mother, Griselda's first problem was solved. Her next problem had to do with the empire she had run for years, and would be even more impactful in her life. She began to suspect that the DEA were almost ready to make a move.

As we've seen, the pursuit of the law was not a new challenge for the Godmother. The blockbuster Operation Banshee was the first large-scale investigation of her business and the source of her wealth, which ended in failure when the New York and federal agents realized she was nowhere to be found. It did, at least, drive her out of the city. The DEA did not give up, and unsurprisingly, the dramatic state of affairs in Miami caused by Griselda's open and flagrant violence drew renewed attention to Griselda and south Florida. In the era of the so-called "war on drugs," the Medellín cartels were attracting attention from some of the highest profile politicians in the country. Around 1981, the federal U.S. government devised and created a special narcotics task force to target the highest levels of the cartels' leadership.

Their bosses were desperate to disrupt the drug pipeline from Colombia and to reduce the sheer volume of cocaine being trafficked into the country. The task force consisted of units from the DEA, U.S. customs, the Coast Guard service, as well as the U.S. Treasury Department. The man at the head of this joint force, the one who everyone reported to, was the drug warrior himself, George H. W. Bush, then Vice President in the Reagan Administration.

To make matters worse, Griselda's own people may have been getting overconfident in their apparent untouchability, thus becoming sloppy as a result. There are accounts that claim that in 1984, as agents of the drug task force were steadily building a case, some of Griselda's sons, likely the younger Osvaldo and Uber, had let slip some sensitive info about their cocaine shipment numbers for that year to some colleagues of theirs. Unfortunately for them, the men turned out to be informants who had been recruited by the DEA. This, combined with Griselda's own boisterous behavior when conducting her business, provided the investigation with plenty to charge, and finally bring down the Godmother. They were very close to being ready to stage their big bust. Griselda likely would have been charged earlier on; however, investigators had been holding out hope that they would be able to directly tie Griselda to several murder charges, the real crime they wanted to nail her for. Although their fortunes would later change, they found no luck at the moment, and drug trafficking charges were all they could muster at first.

Griselda saw the writing on the wall, and she certainly could not run from the law forever. However, federal agents were not the only group that now seriously made her concerned for her safety. Her rivals were becoming more ambitious, and the countless enemies she had made over the years as a result of her brutish killings were eager for revenge. For years, a sense of chivalry that some in the criminal underworld still carried may have allowed her to prosper in relative safety. One of Griselda's biographers, Jennie Smith, argues that at the time, it was generally rare to find narco hitmen who were killing to harm women or children (the restraint that kingpin Tony Montana shows in *Scarface* was not simply there to make Pacino's character more likable). Although some in Miami saw the silver lining in the city's eruption of violence—the fact that it was drug dealers killing other drug dealers—this wasn't the case for Griselda, the woman who some hitmen simply wouldn't take a contract on. This made the Godmother a much more difficult target to arrange a "farewell" for. Just as her femininity aided her during Operation Banshee, with agents struggling to convince their superiors that Griselda was the one worth looking into, it once again came to her rescue during the 1970s and early 1980s as rivals struggled to convince hitmen that she was someone that should be eliminated. However, by this time, Griselda had worn out much of the goodwill that fellow narcos in the industry had toward her, and this sense of chivalry was all but gone as she continued to make enemies in Miami and Medellín. Now, there were plenty of people willing, and even desperate, to kill the Queen of Cocaine.

The most dangerous of these people was a relative of one of Griselda's most famous murder victims. A man by the name of Jaime was looking to avenge the death of his uncle and his 1975 murder. His uncle, at this point dead for nearly 10 years, was Alberto Bravo, Griselda's second husband and the man with whom she had the fabled Bogotá nightclub showdown. The murder clearly did not sit well with Jaime, who was at this point running some kind of criminal organization of his own, very likely following in his uncle's footsteps in the world of narcotics. It's unclear how long Jaime had been pursuing Griselda, but by the mid-1980s, he had found her. He studied her schedule and took note of the places and businesses that she frequented. He was now posting some of his own men as gunmen in some of her favorite shops and malls in the city, simply waiting for Griselda to show her face. She very nearly met her end in Miami.

Griselda knew she was being hunted, and so did law enforcement. In fact, it was becoming a serious issue for the DEA and their investigation. The prospect of nearly a decade's worth of work that they had put into investigating Griselda's cartel being thrown away because of Jaime's grudge was not a welcome one. So, before they made any moves against Griselda, they first had to take care of one of her biggest threats. A DEA agent who was investigating Griselda at the time, named Bob Palombo, explained the dilemma: "It got so bad that we had to interrupt our drug case against Griselda to take Jaime off the streets," (Brown, 2008). It may seem strange that the DEA would expend the effort into protecting Griselda just to have her arrested, but the potential to get further information from Griselda in an official testimony could have been pivotal in the overall investigation into the narcotics trade. Although, much of it was certainly also due to ego. Big busts can sometimes make an investigator's career, as has historically been the case with the New York Mafia's prosecutors, some of whom had even gone on to successful political careers later in life. Regardless of their rationale, they simply wanted to get their man. Or in this case, woman.

Alberto Bravo's nephew and Griselda's most pressing threat were now off the streets, but the Godmother was clearly not home free, and she knew it. Just as the famously eccentric mob boss, Vincent Gigante, had been doing around the same time in New York, Griselda was turning herself into a hermit. Fearing assassins and federal agents around every corner, she had been known to lock herself away in her massive Miami estate for days or weeks at a time, surrounded by armed guards. Apparently, even that was not enough to calm her. They knew where she was, and they'd be coming, eventually. She had to go somewhere. She had to leave Miami.

Flight From Miami

Sometime in 1984, Griselda Blanco fled the state of Florida, the place where she had unleashed the full potential of her aggression, flooded the streets with cocaine, and turned family shopping malls into scenes of spaghetti western-style shootouts that put some of the Mafia's most spectacular killings to shame. This was not much respite for Miami, a city which still had plenty of trouble to deal with, but at least the Black Widow was gone. Griselda was on the lam, but this time she did not return to Colombia. Although the law would have been less of an immediate concern in her home country, she likely knew that she had just as many enemies waiting for her back in Medellín, including several who were potentially still sour over Bravo's death. This time, she fled to California.

Her move to the West Coast was apparently motivated by two concerns. First, obviously, she desperately needed to make herself scarce to avoid death or prison. The other was her desire to penetrate deeper into California's cocaine market, an area that her former apprentice Pablo Escobar had already been operating in for years. Clearly, despite her paranoia and instability, Griselda had lost neither her business acumen nor her ambition and lust for power. California's massive population, with cities that dwarfed Miami, promised even more potential income for her already multi-billion dollar per year operation. California's wealthier neighborhoods in cities like Los

Angeles and San Diego also had a seemingly insatiable appetite for the white powder that Griselda was just so skilled at selling. It would certainly be a lucrative move if the Queenpin could outlast the competition in the Golden State.

Once again, fleeing would not solve Griselda's problems. Unbeknownst to her, although she may have given some of her rivals the slip, the DEA was well aware of her move to California, and the team investigating her followed her right to her new destination. She had set up shop in Irvine, a small city (by Californian standards) near Los Angeles, just past Anaheim. She had herself set up in a nice suburban home with her mother, Ana, who she had brought from Colombia, as well as her youngest son, Michael Corleone Blanco, with whom she had recently been reunited. She had been attempting to make Californian connections while also letting the heat of her Miami rampage die down. She knew, however, that it would not take long for either the feds or her enemies to find her. Indeed, her tenure in California would last less than a year.

In the winter of 1985, when Griselda was 42 years of age, her time atop the world of cocaine came to an end. Caught between rivals trying to kill her and feds trying to imprison her, she was helpless and hopeless. One February morning, the team of DEA agents headed by Bob Palombo, which had followed her trail to Southern California, burst through the door of her Irvine home while Griselda was still asleep in bed. As the story goes, the Godmother was disoriented and severely panicking as her worst nightmare came true. Making good on his promise to his fellow DEA agents, Palombo gave Griselda a big kiss on her cheek just before they led her away in handcuffs. This was a big deal for many, not just Palombo. Another investigator who had been working the case against Griselda was a Miami police sergeant named Al Singleton, another crusader against the cocaine empires in America. She was such a high-profile target that

Singleton claimed she was "our John Gotti" (Corben, 2012), referencing the famous Mafia boss of the Gambino crime family, a man that was highly sought-after by New York police and was finally busted in 1992, seven years after Griselda's initial arrest.

In all likelihood, it was the fact that Griselda had relocated that motivated the DEA to move on her when they did. Now a potential flight risk, they did not want to risk losing her trail and letting her disappear into anonymity in South America. They had her on drug trafficking, but their true goal, what they had been biding their time for, was a charge of murder and an extradition back to Florida, the state she had marred with cocaine and violence for years, to face trial. For the time being, the law was satisfied with keeping her in one place while they continued to investigate her. She was also not extradited to Florida, but rather sent to the low-security women's prison, Federal Correctional Institution, Dublin (FCI Dublin, for short) in a small town in California's East Bay area. Sources disagree on the exact length, but she received a sentence of around 15 to 20 years in prison.

Griselda's arrest and subsequent imprisonment made big headlines. The Queenpin, the most ruthless of the drug lords who plagued Miami in the '70s and '80s, was behind bars. Sometime in late February, the recording of her arrest was televised as news anchors opined about what it may mean for the coke trade in the U.S. No one who watched Griselda be led away in handcuffs on television was more entranced by her story as a man named Charles Cosby. As he listened to the news story about her career, Cosby, who was himself a small-time (compared to Griselda) coke hustler, was blown away by what she was able to accomplish and how wealthy she was able to make herself. He was selling a few ounces at a time here and there, but she was importing hundreds straight from the source. He had simply never heard of *anyone*, let alone a woman, being as successful in the trade as she was. Instantly, Cosby had a new idol.

Cosby, still a young man at this point, had gotten so intrigued by the empire that the Godmother had built that he took the time to write a letter to her while she was in prison, apparently getting in contact with her through a mutual contact that they shared. The two had corresponded, and Griselda was flattered by Cosby's compliments. One day, a shocked Charles Cosby received a phone call at his East Oakland home from prison. It was Griselda Blanco, and she wanted to meet him. Cosby was taken aback—one of the biggest drug lords active in the world wanted to see him face-to-face.

After a series of back-and-forth correspondence, Cosby decided to take the roughly half-hour drive from Oakland down to Dublin, where Griselda was being held. According to Brown (2008), Griselda immediately gave Cosby a hug and a kiss, as though they had been old friends for decades. Apparently, Cosby's praise of Griselda during one of the most difficult times in her life was greatly appreciated. When the two sat down to talk, they quickly got to business. Cosby wanted the life Griselda had, and he needed her help to get it. It remains unclear what her reasons were, but Griselda was receptive to the idea. She knew of his small operation and asked him how much of a supply of cocaine he would need to set himself up for success. Cosby, unprepared for such a question, blurted out the number that came to mind. The meeting was over, and Griselda went back to her cell. Just a few days later, Cosby had a delivery. A Colombian woman handed him some large packages and gave regards from Griselda. Inside of the packages, Cosby found exactly what he had asked for: 50 kilograms of pure cocaine, straight from Colombia.

In one month's time, Charles Cosby went from a middling drug slinger to a millionaire. If he could form a long-term connection with the Godmother of Cocaine, he would be a bona fide drug lord in no time. This wouldn't be a problem for Cosby, as Griselda had clearly taken an immediate liking to him, and she was willing to induct him into her organization. Cosby continued to meet with her regularly while she was behind bars, which was possible because of the lax security of the prison in which Griselda was placed. She found no issues meeting with whomever she desired, allowing her to continue to play a major role in the cartel leadership. In fact, the two soon developed a deep, intimate relationship. Her prison's minimal security came in handy yet again—Griselda allegedly paid her guards $1,500 each per visit so that she and Cosby could be alone to have sex in one of the prison's spare rooms. It's not clear exactly how many conjugal visits they had, but their relationship continued for years. Cosby's magnetic attraction to Griselda and her life was unsurprising for those who knew what she was like. DEA agent Bob Palombo said of her: "she mesmerized people... she could woo you with her acumen and make you a loyal follower" (Simoni, 2018). Cosby was certainly wooed, and it was certainly an unusual relationship.

As the two became closer over time, and as he continued to impress Griselda with his business acumen, Cosby was given more and more control over the cartel. Before long, Griselda had placed him in charge of a large portion of the U.S. side of her cocaine business. For years, Cosby amassed a fortune flying around the country and meeting with Griselda's distributors, arranging deals, and setting up new nodes in the cartel's network. Things were looking good for the new romantic duo, and Cosby had been earning points with the Godmother by spending time with her son, Michael Corleone, while she was behind bars. He had become something of a father figure to the boy, and he was also in regular contact with Dixon and Osvaldo, two of Griselda's other sons from her first marriage, who were by this time integral parts of the cartel's supply network. However, even while behind bars, forces were conspiring against her. Her prison sentence had satisfied virtually no one—law enforcement was upset by the light sentence and minimum security she had received, as well as the rejection of their plan to have her extradited to Florida. On the other hand, Griselda's enemies were upset that she had gotten away with her life. She still had problems to face, and her psychosis was worsening as a result.

Although her rivals would prefer her dead than in prison, they did get a renewed sense of courage, with the Queenpin being out of commission for the time being. Her competitors began going after her underlings and her supply chains like never before, and their attacks were bolder than ever. In 1992, Osvaldo Trujillo-Blanco, son of Darío (or Carlos) and Griselda, was gunned down at a nightclub in Medellín over a debt dispute with some other narcos. Unsurprisingly, Griselda was distraught when she heard the news from her prison home. One of the few people she truly showed affection for in the world was gone, and she vowed swift revenge. Proving that prison was not enough to contain her violent outbursts, she had arranged for Osvaldo's killers to be tracked down in Colombia. When they were eventually located, they were tortured to death.

Griselda had put her rivals in their place for the time being, but the attacks would continue. But ambitious narcos were actually the least of her worries at the moment. The DEA and the joint task force investigating her were working to gather evidence which could potentially eliminate the threat of the Godmother permanently. Extracting Griselda to Florida to face trial for murder, a charge which in that state potentially carried a death sentence, was the holy grail for Palombo and the Miami police department. They continued to investigate her, and what followed was a mix of hilarious and bizarre.

"JFK 5M NY"

Into the 1990s, when the campaign to continue investigating Griselda had picked up steam, the investigating team was continuing to gather evidence in order to slap Griselda with murder charges. The DEA's Central Tactical Program—better known as CENTAC—had been established, and the combined force of the Miami-Dade police and the DEA was known as CENTAC 26, headed by Al Singleton. Created to curb the influx of narcotics into Miami, one of their main objectives was to prevent the Queen of Cocaine from ever stepping back onto the scene. They began using the same tactics that investigation teams in New York City had been using for years. They were aggressively pursuing potential underlings who belonged to larger criminal organizations, and attempted to threaten them with harsh sentences unless they agreed to turn witness and co-operate with the investigation. These tactics were able to make rats out of several famous Mafia members, including Joe Valachi of the Genovese family and Sammy "the bull" Gravano, onetime underboss of the Gambinos. Their counterparts in the south were also soon to hit paydirt.

In a move that was almost certain to doom Griselda Blanco, the feds and CENTAC 26 were able to get their hooks into Jorge "Rivi" Ayala, Griselda's number one hitman and, in many ways, her second in command. The investigation was able to nail down Rivi on murder charges and, facing a possible death sentence, he agreed to tell the prosecution everything he knew about Griselda

Blanco's role in the world of cocaine trafficking. Rivi, is one of the best sources of insight into Griselda's life that is available to us a decade after her death, along with Charles Cosby and Michael Corleone. This insight sheds a bit of light on what Griselda's motivations may have been, and why exactly she was so impulsive in her murderousness. According to Rivi, Griselda simply enjoyed being in constant conflict with her enemies. She took pleasure in organizing the assassination of rivals and would be constantly issuing orders to her subordinates to be on the look out for this person or that person, and to murder certain people on sight. At times, it seems, Griselda was more concerned with eliminating the leaders of other businesses than she was with expanding her own. Whatever effect Griselda's troubled upbringing had had on her, it's clear that she developed into a woman who wasn't just immune to the guilt of taking someone's life. She liked it.

When Griselda was told in prison that Rivi Ayala had turned witness, she allegedly had a severe breakdown in front of Cosby. She knew that of all people, the information that Rivi, her top enforcer, had on her would be more than enough for the DEA and CENTAC 26 to charge Griselda with absolutely anything they wanted. All of her fear and paranoia that may have been quelled by her soft sentence and her confidence in Cosby came rushing back to the surface, and she was a wreck. On the other side, law enforcement could not be happier about the enlisting of Rivi, knowing that a high-ranking rat would be the same death knell for Griselda that it was so often for top Mafia bosses across the country. The Godmother was not willing to give up quite yet. Her mind began racing to hatch a grand scheme to get her out of prison.

In 1994, Miami Sgt. Al Singleton pulled up to FCI Dublin prison with a convoy of police vehicles. He strode into the prison, had staff remove her from her cell, and he escorted her, handcuffed, to one of the idling cars. She was confused and asked what she was being led away for. Singleton told her she was on her way to the airport. She was finally being extradited to Florida for murder charges. When she was told that the prosecution was seeking the maximum punishment—a sentence of death—she had yet another mental break. Time was running out for Griselda to once again slip away from the punishment she had earned.

Sometime in 1995, Cosby again met with Griselda while she was being held in custody, awaiting her trial as the prosecution solidified their case. She was as erratic as ever, cursing Rivi and his disloyalty. Even Cosby, her love and father figure to her child, was worried about her behavior. She was ready to throw her hail mary: She slipped Cosby a note she had concealed which simply read: "JFK 5M NY." It was cryptic, and Cosby had no idea what it meant. She instructed him to pass the note along to Dixon, her eldest son, because he would know what to do. Cosby wasn't satisfied and asked Griselda to tell him what she was plotting. Her plan shocked and disturbed him. She wanted her people to kidnap and ransom one of the most recognizable men in the country: John F. Kennedy Jr., son of the late 35th president of the United States and a member of perhaps the most prominent political dynasty in the history of the country. It was indeed an insane idea, but Griselda was desperate and disturbed. When Cosby expressed doubt over the kidnapping plot, she allegedly became aggressive and violent with him, comparing him to the rat, Rivi. After being thoroughly chastised by Griselda, Cosby reluctantly agreed to catch a flight back to Colombia to rendezvous and pass the note along to Dixon.

Apparently, the plan was to steal JFK Jr. away from his home in New York, hold him hostage somewhere, likely Colombia, if they could manage it. They would then extort the Kennedy clan to use their political weight to arrange for Griselda's release and deportation to Colombia. In exchange, the cartel would guarantee the safe return of JFK Jr. It was ambitious, but it's unlikely that anyone in the cartel besides Griselda actually believed the plan would work. But, for the millions of dollars that Griselda was willing to pay the abductors, she had little problem finding some men to carry out the job. Regardless of his reservations, Cosby was ordered to oversee the plot. He flew out to New York to meet with the people assigned to the job and give them their detailed instructions on what to do and where to take Kennedy when they had him captured. Though Cosby was meant to stay in the city, he quickly fled back to California after meeting with the kidnappers, fearing that if the plot went through, it would draw nationwide scrutiny. He didn't want to be anywhere near the state of New York when it did.

As it happened, the house of JFK Jr. had been staked out for days before any one of the four-man team made visual contact with the target. As the story goes, they finally spotted him walking his dog around his posh Manhattan neighborhood, and approached him calmly. They stopped to speak with him and slowly surrounded him. As luck would have it, a New York police squad car drove by a little way down the street. The captors got spooked and ran, foiling Griselda's last ditch effort to secure her freedom. Though it failed, the existence of the plot eventually came to light and the tabloid magazines had a field day with the bizarre story.

So, Griselda's criminal career ended much like the way it started: with a botched kidnapping attempt. Although her paranoia-induced master plan to win her freedom was doomed from the beginning, her luck had not run out quite yet. As the time approached for her to face trial and what would almost certainly turn out to be a guilty verdict, a scandal emerged that would complicate the trial process and severely hinder the prosecution's ability to validate their case in court. The story is perhaps the most hilariously strange and absurd of the entire saga of Griselda Blanco. Sometime before Griselda stood trial, it came out that Rivi, Griselda's top narco and star witness to the prosecution, had been having regular phone sex with two of the prosecuting lawyers' secretaries during the course of the investigation. Both secretaries ended up being indefinitely suspended after the allegations were confirmed, and one of the women was secretary to one of the lead prosecutors, Katherine Rundle. The scandal rocked the prosecution. Rivi was no longer a viable witness because of the obvious conflict of interest between him and the prosecution team he had been working with. The team could have pressed on with their evidence gathering; however, Rundle in particular was so embarrassed that she preferred to simply get the case over with and out of public attention. They offered Griselda a plea deal where she would serve a maximum time of 20 years (she had received three 20-year sentences, but they were to be served concurrently) in prison with the possibility of early release, rather than the potential maximum penalty in the state of Florida: execution. Griselda agreed and pleaded guilty. The Godmother of Cocaine's reign of terror was over, and Griselda Blanco Restrepo was off to prison for what at the time, could have been the rest of her life, especially considering what her years-long addiction to raw cocaine had done to her body.

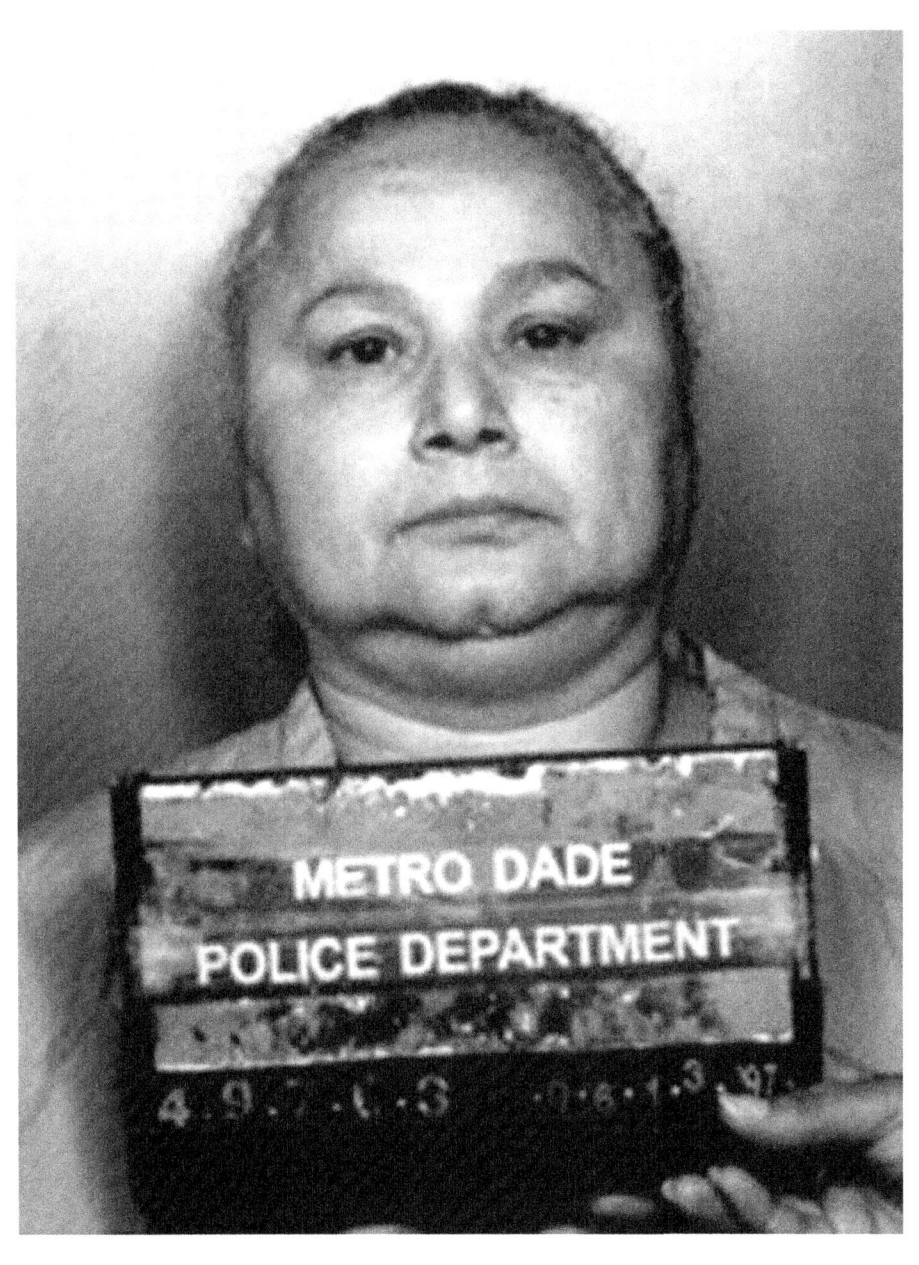

Chapter 7: Legacies

Griselda was finished in the drug trade, but places like Southern Florida and California were still dealing with the repercussions of her life. Around the same time Griselda was sent to prison, Pablo Escobar had been shot dead by police during a botched attempt to escape arrest. Griselda, however, lived on for years until her murder in 2012. The impact of her life, as well as Escobar's, were monumental, and they live on in popular culture and in media like Billy Corben's *Cocaine Cowboys* series. Their careers sparked renewed national interest in the so-called war on drugs and the cities of Miami and Medellín still live in the legacy of the Queen and King of Cocaine.

Homecoming

The decades following Griselda's imprisonment are some of the most mysterious of her life. Her time spent incarcerated seems to have been uneventful, as she was essentially completely removed from the operation of the cocaine empire she had built. When she was released from prison in 2004, Griselda was 61 years old, overweight, and weathered from addiction. Though we don't know much for sure, we do know that Griselda kept two things: grudges and connections. The day she was released, the rat who had turned on her back in the '90s, Jorge "Rivi" Ayala, was beaten nearly to death in prison where he was sent for his part in the murders during the Miami drug wars.

Ultimately, it was decided that someone like Griselda Blanco was not the type of person the government wanted walking their streets as a free woman. She was released on the condition that she be immediately deported to her home country of Colombia. So before long, the Godmother found herself back in the city she grew up in and where she had begun her career. She was by no means poor when she arrived back in Medellín, and, in fact, still had access to immense wealth, more than enough to get herself set up in a comfortable home in the luxurious El Poblado neighborhood. She still earned a passive income from her investments, and the DEA suspected at the time that millions were still spread across her various overseas accounts. She also had very little to fear from Colombian police, as she was no longer in the cocaine trade and did not have any warrants out for her arrest, nor did she face any charges despite her notoriety.

When it was discovered that she was to be sent back to Colombia, many had assumed that the Godmother would last maybe a few days before one of her numerous old rivals got wind of her and decided to settle the score. For years, it appeared very likely that this was exactly what happened. No one had heard or seen from Griselda since her release from prison, and she appeared to drop off the face of the planet. That was until about May 2007, when one of the producers of the *Cocaine Cowboys* documentary received an email from a friend containing a picture recently taken of Griselda, alive and well, at an airport in the capital Bogotá. The image alone was very little to go off of, but it was proof, at least, that Griselda Blanco was still around. By this time, though, it's almost certain that the Godmother, now in her mid-60s, was no longer distributing cocaine. In fact, closer to the end of her life, she had been entertaining the idea of negotiating with TV networks in both the United States and Colombia on possible features about her life. She was retired and living quietly, but she apparently still liked the attention.

Another several years went by without a peep from Griselda or news about where she was or if she was alive. Then in 2012, she was spotted again. One of Griselda's former hitmen, the man known as El Mono, was in the queue at the land registry office in

Medellín in early February. He had recently been released from prison in the United States, where he served time for over a decade. While he waited for his name to be called, a clerk from behind the desk called the next in line: Griselda Blanco. He thought he must have misheard until he saw the Godmother herself get up and approach the office clerk. The last time he had seen her was back in the early '80s, at the party she held at her ranch, at which the four suspected rats were executed. He debated whether or not to say anything to her or simply ignore her and hope she didn't notice him. He decided to greet her just before she left. She was apparently quite happy to see him, and after the reunited pair had exchanged some words, Griselda offered him her new phone number if he wanted to get in contact. Then she left.

It's unclear exactly what Griselda wanted El Mono to get in contact with her for, but he ultimately decided not to find out. Assuming that trouble would be coming her way eventually, he chose to let old relationships lie. It turns out that he had made the right choice. Less than seven months after Griselda and El Mono's reunion, in early September of that year, Griselda was shot dead at the Medellín butcher shop by an unknown gunman. That afternoon, one of the most brutal criminals to plague either Colombia or the United States, was snuffed out.

So Griselda's story ended where it began, on the streets of Medellín. All the years she spent ordering murders and public shootings, kidnappings and armed heists, she survived it all, yet was gunned down in retirement as she bought some groceries. The same technique she had pioneered, the motorcycle driveby, was the same method that took her life. It was almost poetic.

The funeral that was held for Griselda was a strange one. The ceremony itself was incredibly brief, and surprisingly few individuals were allowed to attend and pay their respects. No paparazzi were allowed to attend. It was a small, downcast affair, but the burial afterward was a different story. Still, no photos were allowed and journalists and the press were not allowed to enter to report on the story. Apparently, though, it was one hell of a party. It was complete with mournful dancing, a hefty supply of vodka, and music provided by a mariachi band. Although it surely was not as crazy as some of Griselda's cocaine fuelled bashes of the 1980s, it was probably exactly how Griselda would have wanted herself to go out. Local children were also brought in to pay their respects to the Godmother, who allegedly would return to Medellín every year around Christmas time to distribute gifts to some of the city's poor children.

Today, Griselda is laid to rest in the Cementerio Jardines Montesacro in the town of Itagüí, about a half hour's drive from Medellín. It is the same burial place as Pablo Escobar, and their graves are just a short walk from each other. The gravesites are now famous, if a bit morbid, tourist attractions for the Medellín area. Before she died, the cocaine trade had taken the lives of two of Griselda's sons, Uber and Osvaldo, and only Dixon and Michael Corleone outlived their mother.

Cities in Mourning

The process of recovery for the cities affected by Griselda's cocaine industry and streak of murder was a slow one. Although the operation originally founded by her and Alberto Bravo had operating headquarters in New York City as well as across Florida, in Kendall, Fort Lauderdale, and Florida's capital, Tallahassee, it was the cities of Miami and Medellín that were the hardest hit. Both of these cities still had Pablo Escobar to contend with, but by the early to mid-1990s, the proponents of the American war on drugs decided they needed to attack the cocaine problem at the source. They began a heavily funded campaign to aid the Colombian government in disrupting the supply chain and the leadership of the Medellín Cartel as well as their main rivals, the Cali Cartel. Once Pablo was out of the picture, the cities could begin to heal, despite the fact that future drug lords would still rise to ensure a steady flow of drugs met wealthy American customers.

Pablo's legacy is complex, however. Although he and Griselda brought bloodshed to Medellín like never before, they were both also known for their charity and philanthropic work. Pablo in particular was known for funding and constructing public utilities as well as recreational areas in some of Medellín's poor neighborhoods, where the city's limited budget seldom touched. He was a saint to some, and earned himself comparisons to the fictional Robin Hood, who was a criminal but showed sympathy and charity to the poor. Children in Medellín were able to go to school close to home because of Escobar, who constructed them in areas where the government never bothered. Some believe that Escobar only invested this money, paltry sums for a man as rich as him, as a way to get the city's poor on his side. This way, he would be able to operate easily within those neighborhoods and the police would have no luck in recruiting informants from among the impoverished. This also explains why Pablo and Griselda both paid their lowliest workers quite well, as they did not want anyone feeling taken advantage of enough to drive them to the police. This all may very well be true, but there is no doubt that all the evil of Pablo and Griselda's legacies is mitigated by the fact they were both prolific philanthropists.

Today, Medellín and Miami are very different cities. Miami is now a far cry from America's homicide capital and no longer carries the reputation of drug capital of the world, though the city does retain an amicable relationship with cocaine and many other narcotics. Since the 1980s, no longer do you see near-daily shootouts on street corners or in crowded shopping malls, and you no longer have *Scarface*-style coke lords operating with seeming impunity throughout Miami-Dade county. Last year, the murder rate in Miami dropped another 15% from its numbers in 2020, which were already far below that of comparable cities. The rates are less than half of what they were during the peak of the 1970s and '80s cocaine wars, and Miami continues to go against the trend as other large cities have been seeing growing rates of homicide. Chicago, for example, had seen a 25-year high in murders in the same year. The shrinking total number of homicides in the city is despite the fact that the city's core and the surrounding metro area have grown in population significantly since the 1980s (Lauren, 2022). As a result of the hefty decrease in violent crime, Miami has also seen a return of its once-famous tourist industry. Many elderly residents had fled in the 1980s and its tourist industry was a shell of its former self, but popular media depictions of the city have helped to rehabilitate its image and encourage Americans from all over the country to once again visit and retire to the beautiful seaside Floridian city.

As for Medellín, their recovery has truly been remarkable. For a time, severe civil unrest and guerrilla wars had exacerbated the problems of cartel crime. An insurgent force named Fuerzas Armadas Revolucionarias de Colombia (or FARC) had plagued the country for decades, but in 2016 the guerilla group signed a peace agreement with the government and the armed forces. After these internal problems were over, Medellín has seen record numbers of tourists visit the city, and the tourism industry has grown four times larger since 2002 (Medellín Living, 2019). In fact, it is very likely that the legacy that Griselda and Pablo left behind in Medellín is a major cause of the increase in tourism, along with the drastic decrease in violent crime. Many parts of the city have been "touristified," and the city's tour guides are now extremely well-versed in Escobar's life and history, taking eager tourists through the city to visit some of the famous sites associated with him. One of his former homes has since been turned into a sort of museum or monument by Escobar's brother, Roberto, a onetime bookkeeper for the cartel. The former mansion draws large crowds each year. This is disappointing for some city officials who would prefer the tourist industry to focus on the brighter aspects of the city and its history. It's easy to see why: Many in Medellín still remember what they had to endure in the city during the reigns of Griselda and Pablo, and glorifying these aspects of its legacy can easily re-open old wounds.

The ramping up of the war on drugs in the 1980s under Ronald Reagan was triggered, to a great degree, by the industry that the cartel duo had created. This, too, is a part of their legacy. Because of the fear mongering that took place in the United States over the introduction of cocaine and its sub-product, crack cocaine, sentences became harsher and the criminal code had stiffened considerably. The war on drugs has been a historic failure and has ruined the lives of countless non-violent drug offenders. Many mandatory minimum sentences were introduced in the 1980s for even small amounts of drugs in one's possession. Only now are American politicians coming around to the idea of ending the destructive war on drugs as they begin to see the writing on the wall. Regardless of what the future holds for America's relationship with cocaine, it was Griselda Blanco, a poor girl from the Cartagena slum, that forced the lawmakers of two separate countries to take note of, and seriously reckon with, that expensive white powder.

Conclusion

Griselda Blanco and Pablo Escobar. This was the Royal Family of Cocaine. These two drug lords had built an immense legacy through the decades, and Escobar would go down as the most well-known cartel leader in history. Griselda, overshadowed by the younger Pablo, has an equally complex legacy as the woman who paved the way for the brutal narcos that came after her time and who is seen both as a bloodthirsty killer and as a source of empowerment. Some see her as an erratic, cold-blooded psychopath, where others see a brilliant and strong strategist. Some of the people closest to her, like her youngest son Michael Corleone and her former lover Charles Cosby, choose to see Griselda in a positive light. Cosby spoke of her warm heart and her fierce loyalty to her loved ones, and Michael takes pride in the legacy of his mother, who once dominated a multibillion dollar per year industry.

Griselda's story is truly rags to riches. A street urchin and pickpocket in the slums of Colombia's second largest city, she became one of the most powerful and feared women in the hemisphere. The girl who once ran away from her abusive home and had to lift change off of strangers to feed herself had been bringing in millions of dollars per month by the time she reached the middle of her life. From New York to Florida to California, Griselda built an empire to rival some of the largest Fortune 500 companies in the world. Her second husband, Alberto Bravo, introduced her to the business and gave her access. But she took what she was given and transformed it into something so lucrative that the government of the United States had to intervene to stop it. By these standards, Bravo's operation was simply a sideshow. Combined with Escobar, the chaos that these two sowed was so impactful on American consciousness and the government's war on drugs that it very likely could have impacted the results of American elections during the early 1980s. Drug warriors like Ronald Reagan certainly benefited from the overflow of cocaine into the country and people's fears over the so-called crack epidemic. The drug pipelines established by Griselda years ago provided politicians like these with much to campaign on. Indeed, the ripple effects of Griselda's violence and mass supply of cocaine should not be underestimated.

Michael Corleone Blanco, 44 years old as of 2022, still embodies and embraces Griselda's legacy. Like La Madrina's other sons, Michael became involved in the international cocaine trade from a relatively young age. He only convinced himself to get out and lead a different life in the wake of his mother's death in 2012. Today, Michael operates a self-proclaimed billionaire lifestyle brand named Pure Blanco, which he opened with his business partner shortly following Griselda's murder. The brand focuses mostly on fashion and music, with interests in several other areas as well. The brand also heavily capitalizes on his mother's legacy, with t-shirts and other accessories sporting Griselda's image and catchy, cartel-themed slogans. Needless to say, Michael's life could have ended far differently if he had continued in his mother's footsteps, but is one of the lucky few to have played the game and lived to tell about it.

Charles Cosby, too, was able to eventually exit the business after Griselda's imprisonment and deportation. The two had a complicated relationship, with Cosby once being wounded when Griselda, who suspected infidelity, sent a gang of her people to shoot up his car. After having forgiven any infidelity he may have had, the relationship ended firmly after Rivi's phone sex scandal, during which time it was revealed that Cosby, too, was having relations with a staff member of the prosecution. After this, he went on to become one of the best sources of information we have of the Queenpin, and he serves as the lead storyteller in the profile of Griselda in 2008's *Cocaine Cowboys 2*. During the filming, he was surprisingly open about the intimacy that he and Griselda shared, as well as the inner workings of her business in the mid to late-1980s. He is also possibly the person who had crossed Griselda the most and managed to survive. Griselda knew of his repeated infidelity and did nothing after her sentencing. There was no shootout outside of a packed nightclub, no hit squads sent to his home, and no kidnapping attempts. Perhaps she loved Cosby too much to take his life. Or, perhaps, she was simply sick of murder.

Though the laws and the landscape of cocaine have changed drastically since the Wild West days of the 1980s, Griselda's impact on global narcotics smuggling cannot be underestimated. She was a pioneer in every way. She was one of the first drug lords to ensure she distributed her sources of cocaine evenly so as to never encounter a severe bottleneck in her pipeline. She was an advocate of different, loose narco groups combining resources and connections in order to mutually profit as a cohesive unit. In this way, drug smugglers had access to more resources while also dispersing the associated risk among those involved. It was certainly innovative for its time, and it is believed that this was the beginning of the concept of the organizations that came to be known as "cartels." The pipelines and organizational structures she created remained in use for future narcos for years after she was first sent to prison at FCI Dublin. Indeed, everyone from Escobar to El Chapo, George Jung to Carlos Lehder, owes something to the Black Widow.

Cocaine gave Griselda everything. It lifted her out of poverty in the Medellín slums, gave her freedom and independence, and allowed her to shower her loved ones with everything on Earth that they might desire. Cocaine gave her her legacy and allowed her to create Medellín's own legacy of violence and narcotics. It allowed her to change the social fabric of Southern Florida. And, of course, it made her disgustingly rich. But it also eroded her youthful looks and prompted her to undergo several plastic surgeries in an attempt to stay young. It destroyed two of her marriages and was the basis for two of her partners' deaths. It corrupted her ability to think rationally and stole away two of her boys as well as two decades of her life as a free woman. It was also almost certainly the cause of her death.

Hugo Clark is a Nevada-based author and hobbyist investigator of mysteries, true crime, and crime thrillers. He has authored numerous articles on serial killers and holds a bachelor's degree in Journalism.

References

Alvarez, Jose G. (2012, September 13). Colombia's 'cocaine queen' living in obscurity

    when she was shot dead. *El Pais.*

    https://english.elpais.com/elpais/2012/09/13/inenglish/1347536945_696771.html

Berlinger, J. (2012, September 5). The incredible story of Colombia's 'godmother of

    cocaine.' *Business Insider.*

    https://www.businessinsider.com/the-godmother-of-cocaine-was-killed-in-yeste

    rday-2012-9

Borrell, J. (1988, March 21). Colombia most dangerous city: welcome to Medellín,

    coke capital of the world. *TIME.*

https://content.time.com/time/subscriber/article/0,33009,967029,00.html

Bowley, J. (2013). Robin Hood or villain: The social constructions of Pablo Escobar.

    University of Maine, Honors College, 1-77.

Brown, E. (2008, June 23). Searching for the godmother of crime. *Maxim.*

https://www.maxim.com/maxim-man/searching-godmother-crime/

Burnstein, S. (2020) *Dadeland mall massacre was rooted in drug beef over burglary*

    year before. The Gangster Reporter.

    https://gangsterreport.com/dadeland-mall-massacre-was-rooted-in-drug-beef-o

    ver-burglary-year-before/

Corben, B. (2012, September 4). Griselda Blanco: So long, and thanks for all the cocaine.

    VICE.

    https://www.vice.com/en/article/3b5jz8/griselda-blanco-so-long-and-thanks-fo

    r-all-the-cocaine

Drug Enforcement: The many roles of the DEA. (1993). *U.S. Department of Justice*.

https://www.ojp.gov/pdffiles1/Digitization/147278NCJRS.pdf

Gray, M. (2012, September 4). Griselda Blanco, 'godmother' of cocaine, gunned down in

    Colombia. *TIME*.

    https://newsfeed.time.com/2012/09/04/griselda-blanco-godmother-of-cocaine-

    gunned-down-in-colombia/

Hamacher, B. (2019, July 12). 'Dadeland mall massacre': Thursday marks 40th

anniversary of infamous 'cocaine cowboys' shootout. *NBC Miami.*

https://www.nbcmiami.com/news/local/dadeland-mall-massacre-thursday-mar

ks-40th-anniversary-of-cocaine-cowboys-shootout/127956/

History.com Editors. (2022, April 20). Fidel Castro announces Mariel boatlift. *HISTORY.*

https://www.history.com/this-day-in-history/castro-announces-mariel-boatlift

Jaynes, G. (1981, August 12). Miami crime rises as drugs pour in. *New York Times.*

https://www.nytimes.com/1981/08/12/us/miami-crime-rises-as-drugs-pour-in.

html

Lauren, N. (2022, January 12). Miami-Dade murder rate dropped in 2021 by nearly

15%. *NBC Miami.*

https://www.nbcmiami.com/news/local/miami-dade-murder-rate-dropped-in-2

021-by-nearly-15/2659716/

The History of Medellin. (2019, August 6). Medellinliving.com.

https://medellinliving.com/history-of-medellin/

Meek, A. (2012). Murders and pastels in Miami: The role of 'Miami Vice' in bringing

> tourism back to Miami. *The Florida Historical Quarterly*, (90), 286-305.

Miami metro area population 1950-2022. (n.d.). *Macrotrends*.

> https://www.macrotrends.net/cities/23064/miami/population

Naef, P. (2018). 'Narco-heritage' and the touristification of the drug lord Pablo Escobar

> in Medellín, Colombia. *Journal of Anthropological Research*, 487-502.

Pobutsky, A. B. (2020). Pablo Escobar and Colombian narcoculture. *University of*

> *Florida Press*.

Pobutsky, A. B. (2009). Perez-Reverte's 'La Reina del Sur' or female aggression in

> 'narcocultura.' *Hispanic Journal*, (30), 273-284.

Preston, J. (1982, January 1). New York City, Miami area had record number of murders

> in 1981. *United Press International*.

> https://www.upi.com/Archives/1982/01/01/New-York-City-Miami-area-had-record-number-of-murders-in-1981/6756378709200/

What is Pure Blanco? (n.d.) *Pure Blanco*.

https://pureblanco.com/pages/about

Rennie, D. (2021, December 9). Meet Griselda Blanco, the "queen of cocaine" who ruled her drug

    empire with an iron fist. *All That's Interesting.* https://allthatsinteresting.com/griselda-blanco-la-madrina

Revell, K. D. (2018). God's waiting room: The rise and fall of South Beach as an

    unplanned retirement community, 1950-2000. *Journal of Aging Studies,*

    (46), 58-75.

Simoni, S. (2018). Queens of narco-trafficking: Breaking gender hierarchy in Colombia.

    International Affairs, (94), 1257-1267.

Secretaries suspended over phone sex. 1998, February 24. *The*

    Associated Press.

https://apnews.com/article/d2783734bfb4d93043bae3edec8fbe94

Smith, J. E. (2013). *Cocaine cowgirl: The outrageous life and mysterious death of*

    Griselda Blanco, the godmother of Medellín. Byliner.

 United States v. Blanco, Fact Summary. (n.d.). United Nations Office on Drugs and

    Crime (UNODC).

https://sherloc.unodc.org/cld/case-law-doc/drugcrimetype/usa/1988/united_states_v_blanco.html

Washington Post. (1979, August 13). *The cocaine wars...* Washingtonpost.com

https://www.washingtonpost.com/archive/politics/1979/08/13/the-cocaine-wars/80a37246-219d-4331-9ea0-8c350ee06551/

Wallace, A. (2013, December 2). Drug boss Pablo Escobar still divides Colombia. *BBC.*

https://www.bbc.com/news/world-latin-america-25183649

Image References

Ulises Casarez. (2017, September 6). *Colombia Medellin Landscape.* Pixabay.

https://pixabay.com/photos/colombia-medellin-landscape-2722716/

Jorge Tapia. (2021, January 25). *Miami Bayside City.* Pixabay.

https://pixabay.com/photos/miami-bayside-city-buildings-port-5932835/

Malgorzata Wojcik. (2017, December 17). *Large-Leaved Cocaine.* Pixabay.

https://pixabay.com/photos/large-leaved-cocaine-1091778/

Printed in Great Britain
by Amazon